The Ignatian Way

Simon Decloux, S.J.

The Ignatian Way

"For the greater glory of God"

Translated by
Cornelius Michael Buckley, S.J.

with a Foreword by
The Most Reverend Anthony J. Bevilacqua, D.D., J.C.D., J.D.
Archbishop of Philadelphia

A Campion Book

Loyola University Press
Chicago

Originally published as *La voie ignatienne*
©1983 Desclée de Brouwer from whom permission
has been granted to publish in English.

©1991 Loyola University Press

Loyola University Press
3441 N. Ashland Avenue
Chicago, Illinois 60657

Library of Congress Cataloging-in-Publication Data

Decloux, Simon, 1930-
  [Voie ignatienne. English]
  The Ignatian way: for the greater glory of God/Simon
Decloux; translated by Cornelius Michael Buckley; with a
foreword by Anthony J. Bevilacqua.
    p. cm.
  Translation of: La voie ignatienne.
  Includes bibliographical references.
  ISBN 0-8294-0710-3
  1. Jesuits. 2. Ignatius, of Loyola, Saint, 1491-1556. Exercitia
  spiritualia. 3. Jesuits—Religious life. 4. Spiritual exercises.
I. Title.
BX3702.2.D4313   1991
255′ .53—dc20   90-23986
                                                        CIP

Contents

Foreword

A book about the founding and development of any Catholic religious order contributes significantly to a greater appreciation of the Church for those who read it. Such a book takes on added appeal when it explains the origins of the venerable religious community known as "the Society of Jesus."

The conversion and life of St. Ignatius of Loyola have become the foundation for an institutionalized religious commitment to living the message of Jesus Christ in all its beauty and simplicity. With a tiny band of followers, St. Ignatius forged the beginnings of a community that remains alive today and is attempting to adapt to contemporary society in order to continue its evangelizing mission of carrying Christ to all people.

Through the many changes that have taken place from the time of St. Ignatius until today, the motto of the Society of Jesus continues ever firm: all "for the greater glory of God." It is these changes and how the Jesuits of today attempt to remain steadfast to the intention of their founder while following the call of Christ that is the subject of this book.

The Ignation Way captures the heart of what it means to be a modern-day member of the Society of Jesus. The author does this by including in his work historical data such as how the order actually received the name "Jesuit" by which it is most commonly known today. This practical background information sets the tone and enables the reader to understand the type of service that followers of Ignatius actually perform even to this day.

Any writing on the role of the Jesuits would be lacking if it did not contain an explanation of the *Spiritual Exercises*, which is not simply a book but more a way of life or road that the Jesuit must travel throughout his lifetime. While the Spiritual Exercises of St. Ignatius are not discussed in great detail in the following pages, excellent points are nevertheless offered in important areas such as the "discernment of spirits."

Jesuit studies, education, and culture are given primary emphasis in this book, as well they should. In order to comprehend fully the meaning and mission of this religious order, it is necessary to grasp the motivations for why Jesuits do what they do in the area of vocation training. This logically leads to a discussion on the outward character that Jesuit formation possesses as it prompts "The Companion" forth into apostolic service.

This work also provides important data on other topics such as the purpose of the Jesuit "fourth vow" of obedience to our Holy Father, the distinct charism of brotherhood in addition to priesthood within the Jesuit community, and the double perspective of contemporary Jesuit ministry as "The Service of the Faith and the Promotion of Justice." The role of poverty, both for the individual Jesuit and for the community, as well as the governance of the religious order and the role of superiors are issues that also receive primary treatment.

The beautiful closing chapter examines the Society of Jesus from an ascetical point of view. Excellent insights on a "spirituality of service" are developed, such as the importance of prayer and the Eucharist in all ministerial pursuits and the call for Jesuits to be "contemplatives in action." A simple yet profound synthesis of the twofold purpose of the Society of Jesus is presented: sanctification of oneself and of one's neighbor, all "for the greater honor and glory of God."

As acknowledged in the Introduction, *The Ignatian Way* is an attempt to present what the Society of Jesus can and should be with the grace of Jesus Christ. This book obviously will be of interest to Jesuits and those who work or are associated with this community through its many missionary and apostolic activities.

Numerous observations in this book, however, apply not only to religious or those in the diocesan priesthood but also to the many faithful in the lay state who are striving "to find God in all things." In particular, chapter 5 offers excellent insights concerning growth in the spiritual life that should prove invaluable to those who are serious about developing a strong relationship with our Triune God.

There is little doubt that this book contributes to an enhanced understanding and thus a deeper appreciation of a religious order that has distinguished tradition in the history of the Roman Catholic Church and a continued important place in today's evangelization of, and ministry to, all peoples in our world.

Anthony J. Bevilacqua
Archbishop of Philadelphia

Introduction

This book is written by a Jesuit. The form he has chosen, which frequently reflects his background, is conditioned by what the Jesuit vocation means to him. However, this is not to say that his understanding of "the way of the Society of Jesus," which he has tried to highlight in these pages, will be limited to his own subjective experience. Rather, he also reports, or attempts to report, what so many of his brothers have told him about how the Lord has acted in their lives.

He especially tries to listen to God's call to him as it makes itself heard along the road he has undertaken, even though he is aware that we always fall short of totally embracing the grace that we recognize is being offered to us.

Moreover, what can be said of the life of any of us can be said of a religious order, for like any individual, so, too, a religious order does not always respond to the grace that is being offered to it. It is not always what it *could* be or *should* be; therefore, when we speak in these pages of "the Society of Jesus," of "the companion," or of "the Jesuit," we do not claim to always describe an immediately observable reality. Our treatment will also include the accepted *requisites* for a vocation in the Society of Jesus that—it is important to remember—can be described without attesting to their being always fully realized.

For this reason, the reader should kindly overlook any mode of expression which, if poorly interpreted, could give the impression that the author is guilty of some type of triumphalism. The reality is that the more clearly we recognize the call of grace, the more we— as individuals and as members of a religious order—feel our own insufficiency in comparison to the hope God has for us.

1

The subjective character of this work, which testifies to the limited experience of its author, is hopefully balanced somewhat by the author's repeated reference to a number of objective documents, such as the *Constitutions of the Society of Jesus*, the decrees of the order's Thirty-second General Congregation, and to the letters of the order's former superior general, Father Pedro Arrupe.[1]

In other words, the subjective character of this work should be put into a more objective perspective by the reader's referring to *The Constitutions* and other documents.

Then, too, there are a number of Father Arrupe's letters following the Thirty-second General Congregation (1974-1975) up to 1979 that furnish an outline for many points essential for life in the Society. A list of these documents, published in 1982, suggests a number of themes used throughout this book. Specifically, we note the following:

"Genuine Integration of the Spiritual Life and Apostolate" (1976)[2];
"The Integration of the Spiritual Life and Apostolate" (1976)[3];
"On Apostolic Availability" (1977)[4];
"On Inculturation" (1978)[5];
"On Our Obligation to Meet the Challenge of Atheism" (1979)[6].

ખ ખ ખ

Most likely the name "Company of Jesus" goes back to the year 1537. We learn this from a text of Juan Alonso de Polanco (1516-

---

[1]The general congregation, often called general chapter in other religious orders, is the assembly of representatives from all of the provinces in the order. This assembly has legislative power and makes the most important decisions about the life of the order. Contrary to customs of other religious orders, in the Society there are no set times between general congregations. The Thirty-second General Congregation took place between November 1974 and March 1975, and the last one, the Thirty-third, at which Father Peter-Hans Kolvenbach (b. 1928), was elected general of the Society of Jesus, the twenty-eighth successor of Ignatius, took place between September and October 1983.

[2]Pedro Arrupe, S.J., *Five Recent Documents from Father General Pedro Arrupe, S.J., on Spirituality for Today's Jesuit* (New Orleans: Southern Printing Company, 1980), 1-7.

[3]Pedro Arrupe, S.J., *Selected Letters and Addresses* (edited by Jerome Aixalá, S.J.), 3 vols. (St. Louis: Institute of Jesuit Sources, 1980), 3:111-26.

[4]Pedro Arrupe, S.J., *Five Recent Documents*, 9-19.

[5]Pedro Arrupe, S.J., *Selected Letters* 3:171-81.

[6]*Acta Romana Societatis Iesu*, vol. 17, *fasciculus* 3 (1959), 859-67.

1576), who was a contemporary of St. Ignatius and served as the first secretary general of the Society. Polanco recorded:

> The name is the Company of Jesus. The companions took it before they arrived in Rome. Discussing among themselves the name they would use to answer those who would question them about the group, at that time nine or ten strong, they began to pray and reflect on what name best suited them. Because they had no other leader, no other superior than Jesus Christ, whom alone they desired to serve, it seemed right to them to take the name of Him whom they took for their leader, by calling themselves the Company of Jesus.[7]
> [TRANSLATOR'S NOTE: The Spanish name *Compañía de Jesús* and the French *Compagnie de Jésus* became *Societatis Jesu* in Latin. Hence, "Society of Jesus," the English rendition.]

As for the more popular name "Jesuit," let us reproduce here what Alain Guillermou wrote in the Introduction to his essay in *Les Jésuites: Spiritualité et activités; jalons d'une histoire:*

> The common belief is that the word "Jesuit" took on its pejorative sense after the Society had been founded. There are some people, even learned people, who believe the origin of this sense of the word is to be found during the time of the Jansenist controversies, or later; that is, at the time of Voltaire. Not so at all. As far back as the Middle Ages this word was synonymous with imposture, hypocrite. The origin of the meaning can be traced to commentaries by moral theologians who taught that a man had to show on earth he was a good *christianus*, a good disciple of Christ, so that he could be received on high by Jesus himself, who would have him chosen as another Jesus, a *jesuita*. According to a very normal semantic evolution, however, the term *jesuita* came to be used sarcastically until it eventually took on the meaning of "a false Jesus" when applied to a person who put on airs of devotion. During the time when confession was closely allied to frequent communion, priests were issued a kind of practical guide, called a *confessionale*, which indicated the chief faults a penitent might be guilty of committing. In one such manual of this genre, we read

---

[7]Cf. Dalmases, S.J., Cándido de, *Ignatius of Loyola, Founder of the Jesuits: His Life and Work*, tr. Jerome Aixalá, S.J. (St. Louis: The Institute of Jesuit Sources, 1958), 149.

the typical sentence, *Confiteor me pharisaeum, jesuitam, hypocritam fuisse.* ("I accuse myself of having been a pharisee, a jesuit, a hypocrite.") Hence, the unsavory connotation of the term "jesuit," as I have explained, was used many years before the birth of Ignatius of Loyola. Later the term was resurrected from the past, first in Germany, where the Protestants made a pun on the name *Societas Jesu* and relished addressing the companions of St. Ignatius with the title *jesuitae*. This form of describing members of the Society was also used in France during the same period; however, here the term was not meant to be offensive, and so it was the companions who, out of humility, refused to use it, at least in the beginning. Later, by the time the name had become widespread, the companions themselves were accused of having appropriated the name of our Savior because of how they referred to themselves, and in their defense they pointed out that other religious orders, for example, the Jesuates, had not been blamed for using the name Jesus and therefore the companions should not be singled out for opprobrium. Soon the name became common and was used universally even to the point where, during the Council of Trent, Rome did not balk at employing the term *jesuitae* for the companions who took part in the conciliar proceedings. And, indeed, in 1562 Father Laínez was referred to as *generalis jesuitarum.* Meanwhile, however, the satirical connotation was not forgotten and, as a matter of fact, this meaning can still be found in our modern dictionaries.[8]

In this book we will frequently refer to certain key periods and events in the life of Ignatius of Loyola, the founder of the Society of Jesus. The grace God gave him did not only have a bearing on his own personal way to the Lord, but it also throws light on the essence of the Jesuit's vocation. For this reason, on page 7 we offer those readers who are not altogether familiar with Ignatius of Loyola's biography a brief chronology of the high points in his life to which we refer in the text. We should also point out that in this book we generally use the name Ignatius of Loyola. Sometimes, however, we speak of Iñigo, which was Ignatius's baptismal name (his patron

---

[8]Alain Guillermou, *"Genèse d'une spiritualité: Ignace de Loyola,"* Introduction to *Les Jésuites: Spiritualité et Activités* (Paris: Éditiones Beauchesne, 1974).

saint was an abbot of the Benedictine abbey of Oña-Burgos who died in 1068). Without giving any reason why, Ignatius himself eventually changed his name. Most certainly he had a particular devotion to St. Ignatius of Antioch.

Ignatius Chronology

1491   Probable year of Ignatius's birth

1521   Sustains wound at the siege of Pamplona
       (At this time Ignatius was defending the city in his capacity
       as a gentleman [*caballero*] in the service of the viceroy of
       Navarre. His leg was broken and he underwent a number
       of operations. During his convalescence at the castle of
       Loyola he read *The Life of Christ* and *Lives of the Saints*.)

       Converts; experiences the discernment of spirits

1522   Becomes a pilgrim at Montserrat and particularly at Manresa,
       where he begins to live a spiritual experience and write the
       Spiritual Exercises

1523   Makes a pilgrimage to the Holy Land

1524   Begins studies (Latin) at Barcelona

1526   Studies at Alcalá (arts or philosophy)

       Has unpleasant dealings with the Inquisition, particularly
       because of his apostolic endeavors

1527   Has further conflicts with the Inquisition for the same reasons

       Studies at Salamanca

1528   Arrives in Paris, where he studies (humanities, arts or phi-
       losophy, and theology) until 1535, repeating his studies from
       the beginning

1532   Receives Bachelor of Arts

1533   Receives Licentiate of Arts

1534   Receives Master of Arts

August 15. Vow of poverty (and implicitly of chastity) pronounced by Ignatius and his first six companions at Montmartre.
>   (They vow to go to Jerusalem or, in case they are not able to make the trip, to offer themselves to the pope to be sent wherever he would want them to go.)

1537   June 24. After again spending some time at Loyola, Ignatius is ordained a priest in Venice, along with the five other companions who had not yet received the sacrament of orders.

(Day uncertain) On the road to Rome, at La Storta (16.5 kilometers, or a bit more than 10 miles from Rome), Ignatius hears the Father say to the Son, who is carrying His cross: "I desire that you take this man for a companion," and hears the Son declare, "It is my will that you serve Us." This assurance is given to Ignatius: "I shall be propitious to you in Rome."

1538   Judicial process at the Roman curia, which results in the clear approbation of the companions

December 25: Ignatius celebrates his first mass at St. Mary Major
>   (The departure for Jerusalem was impossible, and so the companions place themselves at the disposition of the pope.)

1539   The first ten companions deliberate about the founding of a new order (and about the "vow of obedience to one among them").

September 3: Pope Paul III orally approves the existence of the Society of Jesus

1540   September 27: Pope Paul III confirms the Society.
        (The Bull *"Regimini militantis Ecclesiae "* limits the number
        of professed to sixty, and the pope approves in general the
        "Formula Instituti " written by Ignatius. This *"Formula"* is
        considered to be fundamental rule of the order and con-
        tains the substance of its rules.)

1541   April 19: Ignatius, elected superior of the Society on April 8,
        at last accepts the office.

        April 22: Religious profession made by all of the first compan-
        ions

1548   Paul III approves the book the *Spiritual Exercises*.

1550   July 21: Pope Paul III issues new Bull confirming the Society
        of Jesus.

        Issuance of the Bull *"Exposcit debitum,"* which modifies the
        "Formula Instituti"

        Ignatius completes redaction of *The Constitutions*.
        (This text is prefaced by the "General Examen" containing
        principles about how to "examine" candidates for the So-
        ciety.)

1556   Death of Ignatius of Loyola

I

Foundations for a Life: The Spiritual Exercises

§1. Vocation: Encounter and Call

As he travels the road along which his life becomes a success or failure, each man—whether he wants to or not—commits himself to something. There are particular moments during his journey when, conscious of his freedom, he is able to see the full extent of the road from where he has come to where he is going. There is also a decisive turning point along this road. It is at this point that he redirects his life toward a new purpose that compels commitment. Such is the story of every vocation.

What happens to the spirit of a person's freedom at the moment when this decision is made? What is the source of inspiration that persuades someone to make a choice affecting his whole life?

We are told that ideas guide the world. Do they also guide the life of each person? And does an idea—or an ideal—determine who will choose the religious life?

This has sometimes been the case, and at times still is. In every choice that pertains to the future, man's freedom presents to him the ideal of what he wants to be before he ever makes the actual choice. And the attraction of giving, renouncing, living a life of poverty and service can of itself invite one to go to where he already knows these human and Christian realities are more easily found and where they can be more readily practiced. For many religious, generosity has been at the root of their vocation, and in no case can generosity ever have been lacking in a religious vocation. But generosity is not enough because what is involved is not an ideal to be espoused, no matter how great the ideal. A vocation is not simply a venture freely undertaken. Essentially vocation means an encounter: a listening, hearing a call from a Person, who clearly makes His presence known; it makes no difference how—imperiously or imploringly, suddenly or expectedly—it is a call from a Person who has a name and who can summon with a word, precisely because He is *the Word*. Today, the same Jesus who traveled through Galilee invites men and women to follow Him. To those He wants and in the way that He wants and where He wants them, He continues to call, "You, follow me!"

Of course, there are many intermediary agents of this Presence that can be given to help a person discover or recognize His call. Jesus' invitation overtakes the person exactly where he is, with all his searchings, discoveries, friendships, encounters, commitments. But the person who enters religious life must at least have discerned that Someone has been waiting for him and has been counting on him to lead a life of intimacy and service.

The choice of the religious life has more in common with an engagement to marriage than with choosing a career, for what matters most is not the work or the tasks to be undertaken but the fact that it is He who asks to be recognized as the Lord of one's life with whom one is to share everything.

Ignatius of Loyola experienced in himself, and in the people he was called upon to help or direct, this gradual yet overwhelming realization of Jesus and His call. He recorded his own experiences in "the choice of a state of life," which he used as a pivotal point in his book, the *Spiritual Exercises*. Here he was thinking of all those people his own experience could guide by helping them see clearly in themselves, by discerning the call echoing deep within them, whether the call was to the religious or to the lay life. When all is said and done, every Christian is called to do what God expects him to do during his lifetime and what He inspires deep within him.

The road taken by each Companion of Jesus shall begin at this state: with the *Spiritual Exercises*, the "school" of St. Ignatius of Loyola. But this stage shall be more to him than the beginning of his journey. From now on the Exercises derived from the book must permeate the whole of his journey. And the Exercises likewise are that privileged instrument which he will use to help others to become what God made them to be, their true selves.

It is impossible to set off along the road of the Society of Jesus without realizing at once the decisive place and role of the Spiritual Exercises. They continuously re-create the interior and apostolic life of every disciple of Ignatius of Loyola.

§2. Love of the Lord Jesus

What are the Spiritual Exercises and in what respect are they characteristic of the "way" proposed by St. Ignatius?

For the Christian, Jesus is "the way, the truth, and the life." He and He alone reveals the fullness of God and promises the outpouring of His Spirit. For this reason every Christian experience is ultimately rooted in Jesus' Gospel, in the discovery of His person and His message. There is no "way" of sanctity or of apostolic service apart from Jesus. For this reason all religious congregations find in the living Word of the Lord the source of their strength, the ever-being-renewed point of departure for that grace proper to their particular religious family.

Moreover, the Gospel offers men and women infinite riches, the very riches of God Himself. The intention of every one of the Church's saints, depending on the historical contingencies of their times or on their own individual spiritual temperament, was to recall this or that emphasis of the inexhaustible Word, or to focus their attention on this or that aspect of Christ's invitation to follow Him. Such has been the way for founders of religious orders or congregations. Such is the way for anyone who chooses to follow them in order to discover the particular accent of Christ's Word that inspired them to respond as they did.

Ignatius of Loyola first conveyed his experience of God and of our Lord in the *Spiritual Exercises*. But the reason he gives for choosing the title of his work might seem stilted, even trite. He writes:

> By the term "Spiritual Exercises" is meant every method of examination of conscience, of meditation, of contemplation, of vocal and mental prayer, and of other spiritual activities that will be mentioned later. For just as taking a walk, journeying on foot, and running are bodily exercises, so we call Spiritual Exercises every way of preparing and disposing the soul to rid itself of all inordinate attachments, and, after their removal, of seeking and finding the will of God in the disposition of our life for the salvation of our soul.[1]

---

[1] St. Ignatius of Loyola, *The Spiritual Exercises: A New Translation Based on Studies of the Language of the Autograph*, by Louis J. Puhl, S.J. (Westminster, Maryland: Newman Press, 1963), [1], 1.

However trite it may seem, in comparing the Spiritual Exercises with physical exercises, Ignatius highlights a practical method that anyone can use in coming to a discovery of God. When we speak of a method, we mean a "route," a "way," or the structure that sets up the encounter. First, it is about this encounter that we should say more before going on to other things, but to *describe* the encounter is not enough. What St. Ignatius is actually talking about in this passage is more a matter of *experiencing* the encounter than of describing it. *The Spiritual Exercises* is not intended as merely a book to be read. To grapple with the Exercises at such a literal level is to risk coming away confused and even disappointed. The Exercises themselves are meant to be a way, a road, composed of various stages that lead to an encounter with God.

This is not the place to develop in any detail the structural make-up of the Spiritual Exercises. Excellent studies on this subject already abound; moreover, for us to undertake such a description would risk compromising this book's stated purpose. One point, however, should be briefly noted: the person who makes the Spiritual Exercises is invited to identify his own will with whatever God's will is for him. This is the end-product that the Exercises aim to achieve. Consequently, a person must first of all free himself from everything that would direct his mind and his heart on any predetermined course and would make him, even partially, disinclined to hear God's call. After assuring himself that he has attained this "interior freedom," a person should then open himself to the possibility of a change of heart that would cause him to look at his sin before the all-merciful and all-compassionate God.

From that point on, the individual making the Spiritual Exercises will have become clearly convinced of his need for salvation and he will be disposed to receiving the grace which saves. He then sets about listening to Christ and contemplating His Gospel. In this encounter with the Lord and through the discovery of His personal call to him, he will find the necessary light to respond concretely to what the Lord expects and wants of him. Indeed, as a result of his contemplating Christ's life and message, the one making the Exercises will focus all his intellect, will, and sentiments on Him who has so captivated him, and, forgetting his own wishes and desiring nothing more than to imitate his Lord in a spirit of love and service, he will center his faculties at that point where he can submit his own will to follow Christ's holy will and that alone. It is at this juncture that he will make his response. Then, led along the road where he hears and receives Him who is the Lord of his life, as He is of all life, he will continue making the Exercises by contemplating Christ's passion, death, and Resurrection wherein he will discover that in the very depths of his being he is profoundly committed to, and absorbed in, the paschal mystery of his Lord, the sovereign power of his life and of the life of every human being.

Such a truncated and hurried sketch of the "four weeks" of the *Spiritual Exercises* that we have given here leaves one open to the charge of failing to present their true nature. However, in such a presentation it is perhaps more important to point out the obvious and thorough Gospel-centered character that distinguishes the Exercises. Ignatius of Loyola discovered the Lord as his one and only master along the route, and from that point on he had no desire to put forward another master to serve. Because, recognizing himself as "the pilgrim," he had to let himself be guided by Jesus along the road of life. It was likewise essential that he find Him at the very heart of his freedom, at the point where decisions are forged in determining the unique history of each person's life.[2] The person making the Exercises therefore discovers that Jesus is found in the dialogue of freedom where His invitation elicits a response; where He makes an intimate revelation of Himself and calls on the one making the Exercises to attach himself to Him; and where, as a result of this experience, the retreatant finds the meaning of his own life. Using his everyday experiences as a background, it is at this juncture that the person contemplates the Gospel in order to discern how he conforms to the truth he has discovered. Jesus alone, "the way, truth, life," can furnish the answer to such a question, not merely in a universal and timeless way, but here and now *for me*. When I encounter Him and focus my attention on Him I am able to place myself at the service of His call.

---

[2] [TRANSLATOR'S NOTE: For the meaning of the term "pilgrim," which Ignatius appropriated to himself, *see* Joseph N. Tylenda (trans. and ed.), *A Pilgrim's Journey: The Autobiography of Ignatius of Loyola* (Wilmington, Delaware: Michael Glazier, 1985), xiii-xv.]

§3. A Way Often Repeated and Continuously Traveled

At the beginning of his religious life—presupposing he has not already made them before he entered—the young Jesuit makes the Spiritual Exercises for the first time. For approximately thirty days, according to the pace laid down by St. Ignatius, he follows the four weeks, divisions within the Exercises which are more or less equal in duration. It is during the course of this soul-moving experience that the man and the apostle of tomorrow is formed. What the retreatant brings away with him is a better knowledge of himself and, even more especially, a better knowledge of God and of the way He leads, which is based on personal experience. "A better knowledge of himself" means the young Jesuit at this juncture of his life will begin a courageous work on his own interior life, his particular habits and inclinations, so as to be better suited for God's work and become better suited for the service of the Kingdom. As for the better knowledge of God and of His guidance: during the course of the Exercises, the voice which the retreatant must hear over and over again, so that he can progress in confidence and perseverance, and so that he can be completely open to His grace, is that of the living and true God, the faithful and compassionate God, who is revealed in Jesus Christ, and who manifests God's countenance and God's voice along the road.

Of course every experience, even a vivid experience, can be easily forgotten unless there is some guarantee that it have a future, that it will be continued in the follower's life. The *Spiritual Exercises* could become just a memory, gradually covered with dust and effaced if, once the thirty days were over, the pages on which they are written were closed forever.

However, if such were the case, the Exercises would not fulfill their purpose in the life of a Jesuit. The Exercises are neither a rocket launching pad nor a fly-by-night fireworks display. They are a school both of prayer and action, a point of reference, a support base to which one returns over and over again because they are a continuous source for deepening prayer and initiating projects. Through the method, described in the *Spiritual Exercises*, one must always come back again to this school of love. Again and again the Jesuit must immerse himself in contemplation of the Lord in order to find light, strength, interior encouragement—or to put it in one of Ignatius's key terms—in order to receive profound "consolation" in the Spirit.

I mentioned "school of love." This is the traditional term used to define the final step in the Jesuit's formation. He makes the "tertianship," or "third year," of novitiate after he has completed his studies but before he begins his apostolate—at a time when he commences to reach his adult stature as a Companion of Jesus. This tertianship, this *schola affectus,* is a time given to spiritual renewal. It is there that the heart of the Jesuit once more has the opportunity to become nourished in its very roots by becoming more intimately attached to the Lord, to the Church he is to serve, to the Society of Jesus itself, insofar as it is the "personal way" to which he has committed himself for growing in love, living in love, and submitting himself totally, joyfully, to the demands of love.

Where else besides in the Spiritual Exercises should one expect to find the center of such a dedicated year in the completion of the Jesuit's formation period? This is the second time as a Jesuit that he makes the full Exercises over a period of thirty days, the period of time St. Ignatius had proposed.

By the time the tertian has completed these meditations, he has grown, has learned more about his capabilities, his limits, as well as the obstacles which threaten his endeavors. The experience of the Lord in his life has become more consistent and also more realistic. The spiritual combat, which he had accepted generously at the beginning of his religious life, has by now, shown him the need for total conversion implicit in such a combat. In tertianship the Exercises of thirty days are made with more conviction, more humility, greater realistic confidence, and also with a love which is both more sensitive and more seasoned. How can any man deliberately match his own strength against Christ and His Gospel and against the total call for conversion it implies, without becoming perfectly aware of his powerlessness, of the impossibility of fending off hindrances that keep him immobile? But then, how can one encounter Christ, "the master of the impossible," without being given the incontrovertible assurance of the efficacy of His grace and of His work, which He brings to bear in those who humbly place their confidence in Him?

The Spiritual Exercises are not the only subject offered in the *schola affectus* and they do not take up all of the time spent in tertianship, any more than they are the sole subject taught in the two years' novitiate where they serve to introduce the aspirant to life in the Society of Jesus. However, the thirty days a Jesuit devotes to the Exercises, first at the beginning and later at the end of his formation, can be considered the most important and decisive times during these two stages of his Jesuit life. According to the very wording used in the *Constitutions of the Society of Jesus,* these thirty days spent making the Exercises are the first "experience" the Jesuit is required to undergo. "Experience," in Ignatian terminology, means an experiment where one is put to the test. Since God is the one who must be first and foremost experienced, who else besides God can give a man the ultimate test for determining his ability to respond honestly to God's invitation?

However, these two decisive stages in the formation of the Jesuit during both the first and second novitiate are not limited solely to making the Spiritual Exercises. Many complementary practices constitute ways to insure the companion's needs along his chosen path. His daily prayer will provide the necessary nourishment to sustain the religious and apostle along the way. During the rest of his life as a Jesuit this prayer will continually renew his ability to hear the Gospel, to encounter Jesus, to discover God. Like every prayer which allows God to draw a person who is aware of loving and of being loved, this prayer will be a prayer of contemplation. It will thus be the illuminated center for a Presence which will not restrict itself to times of formal prayer, but which will tend to be found more and more in the activities, the actions, and the happenings of each day.

There are other spiritual peaks that become part of the Jesuit's day-to-day-routine. The chief one is repeated on a yearly basis when, during an eight-day period, he puts aside all of his work and assignments in order to renew his offering and his service to God by making a shortened version of the Spiritual Exercises. He can make this "retreat" alone or in the company of others. With God's light he can adapt the flexible format to what fits his personal concerns best and where his life is at that given time. But in some ways the retreat will always reawaken the fundamental grace of the Jesuit's vocation, rekindle his statement to the Lord Jesus, revitalize the generous offering of his whole life, and will also deepen his never fully achieved conversion to the unique Spirit of God.

§4. The Discernment of Spirits

The purpose of the Spiritual Exercises is to discover the here-and-now will of God for me and how to conform my life to it. For this reason, the spirituality that flows from the Exercises may be described as the constant search for what God's will is for me.

But where and how does God make His will known? It would be both illusory and naive to expect that every time I do anything God will unequivocally reveal to me all the motivations for my acts. God Himself has given me an intellect, a will, and emotions. Each time I exercise these faculties, which are the sign of His creative presence and the very reason why I am able to respond to His union with me, I function as a person and as a Christian.

In seeking the Divine Will, Ignatius employs over and over again in his writings the term "discern" to signify the essence of this inquiry. Discernment means an enlightened choice, a critical judgment that leads to an appropriate decision. What we will look at here in examining the discernment process are criteria that make it possible for a person to come to such a decision.

From the time I first begin to weigh the alternatives in the course of making a decision until the precise moment of the decision, I experience in myself different inclinations, clear insights, possibilities, attractions. To whom or to what should I attribute their source? In the name of whom or what should I acknowledge my preference for this or that option? During his convalescence while he was undergoing a conversion, St. Ignatius noticed within himself the concurrence of certain thoughts or particular attractions with associated feelings either of agitation or peace. His reflection on these phenomena, which at this time was still rudimentary, later became the point of departure for his teachings on the subject of the "discernment of spirits."

In general, one can say that the discernment Ignatius spoke of implies that during the decision-making process, a person is able to evaluate both *rationally* and *affectively* various options that face him. A rational evaluation involves putting into operation a considered reflection on the different aspects of question in the light of the Gospel and of the values it contains. An affective evaluation consists in paying attention to what Ignatius calls interior movements, which owe their origin either to the good or to the evil spirit. The "Rules for the Discernment of Spirits" instruct us exactly how to recognize (according to the effects they have on us) the work of the good and of the evil spirit.

Since the point at issue here is not Ignatius's theory of discernment, we do not intend to go into detail on discernment as such. But it is necessary to appreciate how important discernment is to those who follow the spiritual way of Ignatius, especially so for Jesuits, the companions of Jesus.

People have sometimes credited Jesuits with having a certain amount of wisdom in solving complicated moral questions or in giving spiritual direction. Whether such wisdom is verifiable or not, to attribute its source merely to the intellectual formation of the Jesuit or to the duration and quality of his studies is to completely miss its nature and its origin. It is the school of practical everyday discernment that is the source of what people perceive to be the wisdom of Jesuits in matters concerning the spiritual and moral life.

To endeavor to discern means to accept the historical condition of man, who is not moved to make a choice on the basis of evidence alone. It presupposes that valid solutions can be given to perceived problems because man has recourse to an inner light that is not confined to the limitations of the ordinary, natural process of reflection. Indeed, this is Ignatius's insight: God is not merely the one to whom I have at one time committed myself or only the One who has spoken once and for all in Jesus Christ; He is also the One who is quietly moving me. He makes His loving activity felt at the center of my heart, my emotions, my passions. Sometimes, when He wants to bring about my conversion or turn me back to what I am meant to be, His action is troubling; at other times, when He sustains my desire for righteousness, supports my impulse for acting generously, encourages my will to serve Him by serving my brothers and sisters, His action is calming and consoling.

Discernment is really the operative principle at the core of the Spiritual Exercises; it is on an equal footing with loving contemplation of the Lord Jesus, who is the source of new desires, fresh insights, a different perspective, and a change of heart in the person who contemplates Him.

If discernment is an ongoing way of life for the individual Jesuit, it is only natural that Jesuits would want to seek ways to practice this same discernment process together in community. This aspect of discernment, which has been present since the very beginning of the order—and most notably in the "deliberation of the first fathers" which settled the question of founding the order—has been frequently recommended during the past few years as a possible means for deepening and renewing the spiritual and apostolic life of the Society of Jesus.

Let it suffice simply to acknowledge here some of the new challenges that such a practice entails. The fact is that being attentive to the Spirit is not to live solely in paying attention to what I, as an individual, experience and in analyzing what my personal options are in a given situation. Community discernment presupposes conversing with others, and it demands I do my best to listen to the Spirit speaking through the reasoning insights of others.

By asserting that community discernment cannot be honestly lived unless a person is willing to put into practice certain indispensable spiritual conditions for seeing clearly God's will, we emphasize that it is more difficult than practicing individual discernment where such conditions play a lesser role. However, all discernment aims at attaining interior freedom unimpaired by any prejudices and free from all spontaneous reactions. Whenever I practice any type of discernment, I must neutralize those tendencies within my being and in my freedom that are not in accordance with the Gospel. I must accept and fix my gaze and my heartfelt attention on the Lord of the Gospel alone and humbly pray to receive His light. And finally when it comes to communal discernment, I must ask Him to confirm whatever increasingly appears to correspond more to His call at the present and live in anticipation of His future grace.

§5. Purity of Intention

All should make diligent efforts to keep their intention right, not only in regard to their state of life but also in all particular details. In these they should always aim at serving and pleasing the Divine Goodness for its own sake and because of the incomparable love and benefits with which God has anticipated us, rather than for fear of punishments or hope of rewards, although they ought to draw help also from them. Further, they should often be exhorted to seek God our Lord in all things, stripping off from themselves the love of creatures to the extent that this is possible, in order to turn their love upon the Creator of them, by loving Him in all creatures and all of them in Him, in conformity with His holy and divine will.[3]

---

[3] Saint Ignatius of Loyola, *The Constitutions of the Society of Jesus*, tr. George E. Ganss, S.J. (St. Louis: The Institute of Jesuit Sources, 1970), Part 3, chapter 1 [288], 165.

Note the extreme urgency of this recommendation that Ignatius directs to his brother Jesuits in the third part of the *Constitutions of the Society of Jesus*. In the *Spiritual Exercises,* he likewise writes: "In every good choice, as far as it depends on us, the eye of our intention must be simple."[4] I must adjust my vision, which may be faulty or unreliable until it is perfect. This way of thinking, as Ignatius has described it, emphasizes the nature of that interior freedom that has to be the basis of all discernment and of every choice, as indeed it is of every action.

There is a fundamental perception we should not lose sight of here. Ignatius places it at the beginning of the *Spiritual Exercises* and without it, it is vain to seek God's will. Basically, this perception can be summed up as a recognition and acceptance on our part of God's total uniqueness. He alone is worthy of being chosen and loved for Himself. The goodness, which He manifests in His creation, and the offering to us that He makes in His covenant, as well as the personal invitation He extends to each person, justifies our unreserved attachment to Him. All of created reality, on the other hand, is offered to man as subordinate to his attraction for God and it becomes relative in respect to this one absolute choice.

If true spiritual freedom consists in accepting God's unique sovereignty, it is clear that this freedom is the result of a conquest, and of a transformation, which ultimately God alone can bring about in our hearts. Is it necessary to be an outstanding expert on the human heart in order to discover the continuous activity of conscious motivations and more or less subconscious motivations that underlie and accompany our decisions and our actions? What about self-interests that are more or less clear, what about needs in which the ego seeks and finds itself, what about complex desires that have to be recognized and outwitted!

The objective Ignatius proposes in the passage cited above does not consist primarily in the analysis of feelings but rather in the simplification of our affective life and in the reinforcement of our free

---

[4] *Spiritual Exercises* [169], 71. [TRANSLATOR'S NOTE: The original Latin reads *"In omni bona electione quantum est ex parte nostra oculus intentionis nostrae debet esse simplex . . ."* The Puhl translation, which is used in this volume, reads: "In every choice, as far as depends on us, our intention must be simple . . ." Puhl does not give a literal rendition to the expression *oculus intentionis* "eye of the intention," or to *bona electione* "good election," which Father Decloux stresses in the French text.]

impulses toward God. A deeper knowledge of self in the light of God is necessary in all of this process, but of even greater importance is the gift of the Spirit, which can purify, heal, and integrate.

Father Louis Lallemant (1587-1635), a tertian director at the beginning of the seventeenth century, developed extensively the idea of the need for "purity of heart" and for "a docility to be led by the Holy Spirit," which is referred to in *The Spiritual Doctrine of Father Louis Lallemant,* a book compiled from manuscript notes of his conferences and *pensées* by his tertians.[5]

> To be able to conceive how requisite purity of heart is to us, it would be necessary fully to comprehend the natural corruption of the human heart. There is in us a very depth of malice, which we do not perceive, because we never seriously examine our own interior. If we did, we should find therein a multitude of desires and irregular appetites for the honors, the pleasures, and the comforts of the world unceasingly fermenting in our heart.[6]

And Father Lallemant is not content to suggest that we merely study these negative tendencies of our being. He also emphasizes how important it is that we keep them so that God may be made present in us by means of the gifts of His grace or through our apostolic endeavors. To appropriate to ourselves what can only be the work of God is, assuredly, to go contrary to purity of heart, to an honest and unselfish intention, to that radical disposition of complete abandonment of self to the will of God, without which the religious and the apostle cannot sincerely offer himself to divine grace.

When Father Lallemant takes up the subject of purity of intention, he points out for us its principal obstacles: "vanity, pleasure, self-interest, aversion." Therefore, to grow in the freedom of the Spirit one must be purified from these spontaneous and sometimes subconscious sentiments. This process of purification corresponds in general to the work of the first week of the Spiritual Exercises, which is "to dispose the soul to rid itself of all inordinate attachments."[7]

---

[5]These are the third and fourth of seven principles of Louis Lallemant, S.J., *The Spiritual Doctrine of Father Louis Lallemant of the Society of Jesus,* edited by Alan G. McDougall (Westminster, Md.: Newman, 1928), 80-179.

[6]Lallemant, *Spiritual Doctrine,* 81.

[7]*Spiritual Exercises* [1], 1.

Then, when he writes about the guidance of the Holy Spirit, he refers us directly to the dynamic of the second week of the Exercises that culminates in the "election," at the point where the Exercises prepare us "to seek and find the will of God in the disposition of our life for the salvation of our soul."[8]

Even if the spiritual doctrine of Father Lallemant is described here as a goal difficult to reach, it does show us clearly the direction of the road which leads to a discernment that conforms more and more to God's action in us.

> The end to which we ought to aspire, after having for a long time exercised ourselves in purity of heart, is to be so possessed and governed by the Holy Spirit that he alone shall direct all our powers and all our senses, and regulate all our movements, interior and exterior, while we, on our part, make a complete surrender of ourselves, by a spiritual renunciation of our own will and our own satisfaction. We shall thus no longer live in ourselves, but in Jesus Christ, by a faithful correspondence with the operations of his divine Spirit, and by a perfect subjection of all our rebellious inclinations to the power of his grace.[9]

What Father Lallemant describes here corresponds to the perfection of the Christian life itself and so it is not a way reserved exclusively for the members of the Society of Jesus nor even for those who are inspired to follow the path of St. Ignatius of Loyola. The text we have cited, however, recalls certain tones which are in harmony with God as He is experienced in the unfolding of the Spiritual Exercises; and, most especially, are these tones in tune with the apostolic life, which enjoys a central place in the vocation of the Jesuit, as we point out later in this book.

§6. Third Degree of Humility

Many people are aware of those pages from the *Fioretti* in which St. Francis of Assisi defines "perfect joy": that joy, which the world cannot give, in which the person in love with Christ, experiencing

---

[8]Ibid.

[9]Lallemant, *Spiritual Doctrine*, 113.

humiliation and rejection, finds himself united with his Lord by reliving in some way the drama of Christ's Passion in himself, or by having Christ relive in him His own rejection by people.

In a plain style, clearly bereft of all the poetic grace and charm of the *Fioretti*, Ignatius of Loyola defines with remarkable precision a similar procedure in his *Spiritual Exercises*. Indeed, it is in this part of his book that he invites the retreatant to consider three possible degrees, or modes, of humility.

Humility is not used here in the sense of one moral virtue among others. It qualifies the degree of detachment or of complete forgetfulness of oneself which the contemplation of the Lord Jesus allows one to attain. In this sense, then, humility, as Ignatius defines it, is the invasion of Christ-forming grace, but considered from a different point of view; it is the same love which unites the person so closely to Christ as to make him want to identify his will with the will of his beloved Savior.

The first two degrees of humility presuppose that one has given up sin so that the glory of God can triumph in him; the third degree follows from a logic of wanting to do even more, of wanting to emphasize the power of the total selflessness of love. The exuberance of feeling that dwells within the person who prays in this way is really a sudden spontaneous craving for the glory of God; but it is a glory that is focussed completely on the countenance of Christ, that allures him to follow in the kenosis—in the mystery of Christ's discarding the manifestation of the majesty, power, and glory that belonged to Him as God in order to become man and savior, the mystery of his total abasement.

> The Third Kind of Humility. This is the most perfect kind of humility. It consists in this: If we suppose the first and second kind attained, then whenever the praise and glory of the Divine Majesty would be equally served, in order to imitate and be in reality more like Christ our Lord, I desire and choose poverty with Christ poor, rather than riches; insults with Christ loaded with them, rather than honors; I desire to be accounted as worthless and a fool for Christ, rather than to be esteemed as wise and prudent in this world. So Christ was treated before me.[10]

---

[10]Ignatius of Loyola, *Spiritual Exercises* [167], 69.

There is not the slightest trace of masochism in such an interior disposition, in such a loving impulse from the heart. Suffering here does not have a value in itself or in some perverted pleasure it can cause. What is meaningful here is not suffering, poverty, humility and contempt; but Christ suffering, poor, humble and despised. The driving force that moves the one who prays this way is that love which strives to resemble Christ and to partake in His sufferings for no other reason but love itself. In other words, it is the affection, which is at the same time respectful and loving, for the person of God revealed in his Son Jesus.

This page from the *Spiritual Exercises* has a special place in the quest for finding the will of God. It is at this juncture in the retreat when the person, who is getting ready to specify his "election," decides on what course and direction he will take in response to God's love for him and to the invitation God extends to him. The "consideration" of the three modes of humility should in some way prepare the will of the person who wants to act solely in accord with God's will. The recollection of Christ poor and humiliated should be the sole criterion and assurance of what is going to keep him faithful to who he is in deciding on the choice he is about to make.

From that moment on, the rule of truth is the equivalent of his conformity to Christ. When Ignatius drafted the text for those who are being examined as candidates for the Society, he explicitly recalled this rule and made it an inspiring principle for the Jesuit's whole life.

For this reason it is appropriate here to cite this text taking note of both the endearing and the unyielding imagery it contains. Ignatius does not contrast the spirit of the world with the spirit of Jesus in order to make a contemptuous judgment on the world, nor is he motivated by a rigorous type of voluntarism. Neither is he concerned with giving his sons, who must face the dangers of the world, a rule that will safeguard their purity. No, by giving them the opportunity to be taken up with, and captivated by, the contemplation of Jesus he once again invites them to be converted. The beginning of this Ignatian text emphasizes how important it is for the spiritual life and for the progress one wants to make in it to accept sincerely and to desire ardently what Jesus proposes and reveals. Indeed, apart from Jesus there can be no other path leading to true life.

It is likewise highly important to bring this to the mind of those who are being examined (through their esteeming it highly and pondering it in the sight of our Creator and Lord), to how great a degree it helps and profits one in the spiritual life to abhor in its totality and not in part whatever the world loves and embraces, and to accept and desire with all possible energy whatever Christ our Lord has loved and embraced. Just as the men of the world who follow the world love and seek with such great diligence honors, fame, and esteem for a great name on earth, as the world teaches them, so those who are progressing in the spiritual life and truly following Christ our Lord love and intensely desire everything opposite. That is to say, they desire to clothe themselves with the same clothing and uniform of their Lord because of the love and reverence which he deserves, to such as extent that where there would be no offense to His Divine Majesty and no imputation of sin to the neighbor, they would wish to suffer injuries, false accusations, and affronts, and to be held and esteemed as fools (but without their giving any occasion for this), because of their desire to resemble and imitate in some manner our Creator and Lord Jesus Christ, by putting on His clothing and uniform, since it was for our spiritual profit that He clothed Himself as He did. For He gave us an example that in all things possible to us we might seek, through the aid of His grace, to imitate and follow Him, since He is the way which leads men to life. Therefore, the candidate should be asked whether he finds himself in a state of desires like these which are so salutary and fruitful for the perfection of his soul.[11]

The Jesuit—no longer only the candidate for the Society of Jesus—who reads this text over and over again and who uses it to gauge how he lives up to the grace of his vocation, becomes aware at each reading of the indescribable gift it contains. When he confronts the trials and struggles that come his way, when he becomes the object of misunderstandings and false accusations, he first examines his conscience and his conduct to determine if there is any possible fault on his part, and then he begins to give thanks to God and to praise Him for what He has given him, often in a very small measure: fellowship with his beloved Savior through humiliation and disgrace in the eyes of men.

---

[11]Ignatius of Loyola, "General Examen," *Constitutions* [101], 107-8.

And if there are times when he avoids encountering such affronts and false accusations, he thanks God for having pity once more on his weakness. At the same time he uses the occasion to examine himself on the purity and sincerity of his commitment.

However, we must recognize the fact that most of the time we breathe this air of the third degree of humility only from afar. This fact in itself offers us the opportunity to humiliate ourselves more because of the meagerness of our love and to abandon ourselves to the guidance of Him who alone knows what is good for us.

In a similar text, that is to say, when Ignatius of Loyola deals with those who shy away from a real desire to unite themselves with Christ poor and humiliated, he speaks of the advantage of at least having the "desire of the desire" for this union.[12] Yes, Lord, if my heart is fearful, if my will hesitates, if I feel disconsolate rather than consoled by the thought of sharing in Your sufferings and humiliations, do not think that the weakness of my desire and of my love are my last word in the matter and the place where I shall remain at rest. An uneasiness continues to dwell within me; I await strength and generosity, which, sadly, I do not now recognize within myself, and which will bring me closer to Your side without any boasting or without any foolish personal gratification, but with the loving affection and humility of one who abandons himself to You and learns from You all he knows about God and man.

§7. Other "Experiments"

Making the Spiritual Exercises which grew out of Ignatius's prayer at Manresa is only one of the saint's experiences that the young Jesuit is asked to reenact at the beginning of his religious life. He is also given other "experiments" designed to establish a solid foundation upon which he can build up his confidence in God, fortify his humility and desire to be at the service to the Word, and intensify his encounter with the suffering Christ.[13]

---

[12]Ibid. [102], 108-9.

[13]"Experiments": We have used this consecrated term in the traditional vocabulary of the Society of Jesus, even though the [French] translation of the *Constitutions* made by Father Courel renders this *Ignatian* term "experiences." François Courel, ed *and tr., Les Constitutions de la Compagnie de Jésus.* Collection Christus (Paris: Desclée De Brouwer, 1967), 23-24. [TRANSLATOR'S NOTE: In his English translation of the *Constitutions*, Father George Ganss also employs the term "experiences" rather than "experiments."]

Experiments are outlined in the text from the "General Examen" which should be proposed to all who request admission into the Society (Nos. 73-77). The order for the experiments is as follows: The thirty-day Spiritual Exercises, service in the hospitals, the pilgrimage, performance of humble functions in the house, teaching Christian doctrine and (for the priests) preaching and hearing confessions. But it is explicitly stated that these experiments "may be gone through in whole or in part throughout the entire [two years] of a candidate's probation, with sometimes some of the [experiments] and sometimes others coming earlier, as seems expedient in our Lord."[14] Different experiments also ought to be made, or remade, during the third year of the novitiate (tertianship). However, I shall not consider in this book all of the experiments Ignatius recommended, for they are not of equal importance. Their specific value can be determined on an individual basis once the needs and background of each person are understood.

In addition to making the Spiritual Exercises, going on a pilgrimage for a month—or for a shorter period of time as is often the case—is likewise reliving one of Ignatius's experiences. Is not the title of his autobiographical account in which he has described for us his years of conversion "The Story of the Pilgrim"? And, when speaking about himself in this part of his autobiography, does he not prefer to use the third person singular, "the pilgrim," rather than the first person singular? From the time immediately after his conversion, when God started him on his way and until that day when he found how he could best work in the service of the Church, Ignatius traveled over roads in the guise of a pilgrim. He pressed forward, drawn only by his faith and his confidence in God, and then, refusing all other security, he abandoned himself to the charity of God and men.

However, Ignatius's wandering itinerary would not in itself be enough to justify a pilgrimage experiment for a young Jesuit. A search for an analogous spiritual experience must be added to the outward imitation of Ignatius's travels, undertaken as they were under conditions in every way different from those undertaken today. What Ignatius experienced and perceived while traveling like a

---

[14]*Constitutions* [71], 98.

pilgrim and a beggar is, it seems to me, what young Jesuits are expected to rediscover in the pilgrimage experiment. What this is can be summarized under the following headings: a discovery of freedom and mobility, that later on are connected to his Jesuit apostolate; a confidence in God's way of leading him, as well as the ability to display that confidence by a humble dependence on those who furnish him with food and lodging; a conviction that he should not rely on himself for supplying future needs; a greater awareness that he will be entering a world where the exchange of ideas through easy conversing and dealing with others is taken for granted; an attachment to actual poverty which comes about by entrusting one's self into the hands of other people and God; an introduction to the kind of prayer that accompanies one and sustains one during the course of each day's journey. Moreover, there is the physical exercise to which the body must submissively endure. This can have the effect of fostering a spirit of interior poverty and at the same time it endows the Jesuit with a flexibility that consists of an unassuming attitude in his encounter with God and men. Traditionally, religious life has always emphasized the importance of a regulated schedule of physical exercise and of bodily discipline in growing to receive the Spirit. Here, the exercise the pilgrim undertakes works differently from that practiced by monks in their monastic daily order. If the purpose of the gentle yet constant monastic regime is to subordinate desire to the supremacy of the Word and of God's praise, the walking exercise of the pilgrim is primarily designed to impart to him deep-seated attitudes, which later on will distinguish him as an apostle. These dispositions of mind were described in Jesus' advice to the disciples when he sent them on mission:

> Provide yourselves with no gold or silver, not even with coppers for your purses, with no haversack for the journey or spare tunic or footwear or a staff, for the workman deserves his keep. Whatever town or village you go into, seek out someone worthy and stay with him until you leave. As you enter his house, salute it, and if the house deserves it, may your peace come upon it; if it does not, may your peace come back to you.[15]

---

[15]Matthew 10:9-13.

The experiments of working in hospitals and of teaching Christian doctrine are also rooted in the experience of Ignatius and his first companions. Immediately before the foundation of the Society of Jesus, all of them had come to Italy with the intention of sailing together for the Holy Land. In the meanwhile, however, they fanned out to a number of towns and began exercising their priestly ministry, in which teaching catechism, placing themselves at the disposal of the poor, and serving the sick played a central role.

At a later date, when Ignatius gave instructions to the Jesuits who were going to the Council of Trent, he did not fail to remind them about both teaching catechism to children and the importance of serving the sick in the hospitals. Moreover, in the very formula of profession which the Jesuit pronounces at the time of his final and public commitment to God in the Society, he makes particular mention of the "instruction of children." Further on in this same vow formula he promises to show "special care" for "children and uneducated persons." This "holy practice" is justified by a twofold reason: "the outstanding service which is given through it to God our Lord by aiding the souls which belong to Him," and the greater danger of its "being allowed to fall into oblivion and dropped" in favor of "other more conspicuous services such as preaching and the like."[16]

We can see from this instruction that there is nothing more contrary to Ignatius of Loyola's experience and thinking than a priesthood restricted to working with the intellectual and socially elite. This truth is even more evident when we consider the fact that the group of "reformed priests" which was what the Society of Jesus was called in its earliest days, was determined to correct certain commonly held deviations within the priestly ministry in terms of personal security or a desire for self-fulfillment. Later in this work I shall speak of how the priestly heart of the Companion of Jesus ought to be open to every situation which gives promise of having a need for salvation. Speaking here of the experiments that the novices perform, it seems to me it is important to stress one more point: at the time when the interior man and the apostle is being formed, it is most important that the novice be in touch with men and women who

---

[16]*Constitutions* [527-28], 238-39.

await salvation, that is, with those who are suffering; with those who do not know where to turn; with those who are led astray, sometimes despite themselves; with those who feel they are at the end of their rope; in short, to be in touch with the very heart of the paschal mystery of Jesus. This being "in touch with" is very different from a simple theoretical contact, from the desire to know better about those who suffer; essentially this former type of contact consists in being at the disposal of those who suffer; it is for them a "ministry," a fraternal dialogue during which they are offered the sacraments of the Church, which alone are capable of signifying to every person, and especially to those who are suffering and dying, their ultimate worth and dignity, a worth and dignity which is nothing less than the materialization of Christ Himself.

Another experiment deals with performing the ordinary work around the house (and in his writings Ignatius loves to come back to the subject of waiting on table and helping the cook). "New" experiments are often proposed to young Jesuits today because the list of experiments recommended by Ignatius is an open list, which necessarily ought to be adapted to current situations in which the man really undergoes a formation experience, one that will also have an influence on molding the apostle of tomorrow. This ideal can come about by the young man's sharing an extended period with the physically or mentally handicapped during a prolonged hospital experiment. It can also be achieved by doing manual work in a factory. In this type of experiment, young novices can be introduced to real life situations and thereby experience firsthand a social behavior and a human environment, which they might otherwise have not experienced.

Thus little by little the dispositions of the apostle are impressed upon the companion's soul along with the "solid virtues." These dispositions correspond to the same sentiments as those of Jesus Himself, sentiments the Gospel reveals to us as being nothing short of an overwhelming "philanthropy"—a love of mankind.

§8. An Instrument for the Apostolate

This chapter, which focusses on the first steps in the formation process, has highlighted the crucial role of the Spiritual Exercises in the life of a Companion of Jesus.

However, it is important to remember that at the time when Ignatius decided to take others through the steps that God, his true "schoolmaster," had used to form him, the Society of Jesus did not yet exist. Moreover, the Spiritual Exercises proved to be the means Ignatius used to recruit his first companions, one after another, and had them join him in a project whose structure would only gradually take shape. Yet, at the same time, the Spiritual Exercises have always been an apostolic means for helping one's neighbor.

In the same sense, from the beginning the Exercises were not meant to be only for the Society of Jesus but rather for the whole Church. And indeed they have continued to be used in this same way from the days of Ignatius right up to our own time.

From this point of view, the relationship of the Society to the Spiritual Exercises is one of responsibility. It was responsibility that Ignatius felt toward his neighbor, particularly after his return from Jerusalem, when he began to sense more accurately the call to "help souls." The way he took on this apostolic responsibility was by faithfully transmitting to others what God had entrusted to him. Ignatius, therefore, had to recognize in the grace he had received at Manresa a more universal grace. The steps that led him to his unmistakable encounter with the God of Jesus Christ were the steps he would offer to others. By inviting other people to follow the successive stages along the same road he had traveled, he enabled them to let God also link up with their feelings, moving them on to a radical conversion, drawing them closer to His will and to His love. Not only does the interior life of the Society of Jesus and of each Jesuit spring from the Spiritual Exercises, but so also does the enthusiasm—and, in some way, the fundamental approach—of the Jesuit's apostolate.

Ignatius's progression from the Exercises to the apostolate was not unique. Every Jesuit likewise goes from his own personal experience with the Spiritual Exercises to aiding his brothers and sisters through the Spiritual Exercises, which somehow furnish him with a point of reference and a source of privileged inspiration. This fact was verified among the first generation of the companions. Ignatius very much approved of the way in which Peter Favre, his first companion at Paris, gave the Exercises.

The example of Peter Favre is particularly enlightening because in comparison with Ignatius he had a very different kind of apostolate and style of giving spiritual direction, and yet he was able to use this

"Ignatian instrument" with noteworthy success. We can say that such is still the experience of Jesuits today.

Formed by the Spiritual Exercises and so profoundly touched by this experience that it continues to influence his own prayer and actions, today's Jesuit will give retreats to others, using as needed, a number of different ways of presenting the material of the Exercises to accommodate people of different backgrounds. Retreats can be considered the special gift the Spirit continues to give to the Church through Ignatius of Loyola and the Society of Jesus. The Jesuit will also help his brothers and sisters to find God in their own prayer, a prayer oriented toward conversion, discovery, and acceptance of the will of God in their lives. Many Jesuits, even those who are normally involved in all sorts of works other than giving retreats, regularly devote a certain amount of their time, even their vacations, to making known to others the grace of the Exercises, a grace which has been for themselves such a pivotal experience.

But this fraternal aid is not offered only within the context of a retreat. The grace of the Exercises is in itself more extensive and simple as well as capable of being passed on and understood beyond the framework of a formal retreat. Through his spiritual conversations or by his written correspondence, the Jesuit will often act as a servant to the grace he himself has received for the good of the Body of Christ, just as Peter Favre and Ignatius of Loyola did. How do I hear God so that I can become converted and can embrace His will? That indeed is the fundamental question which lies deep in the heart of every Christian and it expresses itself according to each person's unique personality and background. Because the Jesuit is a man who has been schooled in spiritual discernment by the Exercises, and because he has been thoroughly trained to contemplate Jesus, whom he wants to make more and more the light of his intelligence and the inspiring strength of his decisions, he perceives this fundamental question as well as the specific way it translates itself in those whom he directs. But with humility and patience, without force and without wanting to substitute himself for the one and only Savior Jesus Christ, he is content to allow the person's meditation to progress independently of his own way of looking at things and of his own suggestions. Now and then he will help a person see clearly into himself or will have to reveal to him the hidden spot where his interior struggle is taking place. This insertion might mean giving the person a healthy spiritual jolt, or on the contrary, it might entail comforting him, putting him at peace, or being for him the witness of God's mercy.

The insight that he has gradually acquired in himself and in his own experiences gives him the ability to do all of this; it enables him to unravel with greater dexterity the nets which fetter his struggling brothers and sisters who want to be helped and enlightened.

As we see, if the Spiritual Exercises are for the Jesuit an "instrument" of unequaled value in the apostolate, they do not acquire this effectiveness unless they have been previously ingrained in the innermost recesses of the soul of whoever wishes to use them with profit. The text of the Exercises in itself, however, remains a unique method recommended by St. Ignatius of Loyola for the person who wants to set off on the strenuous road of conversion, of seeking God and finding union with Him. But also, in a broader sense, the Exercises can inspire and motivate in an endless variety of ways the ministry of spiritual direction, and of conversing and dealing with others at a fraternal level—activities which take place every day in the lives of the Companions of Jesus.

II

Studies, Education, Culture

§1. Studies

After the first years of religious life in the Society, the novice takes vows which, as far as he is concerned, are final. He commits himself to lifelong poverty, chastity, and obedience to God, and he promises to follow His way in the Society of Jesus, so that from then until death he will take part in the apostolic work of the Society.

The years of formation are years of testing and, as such, they can present the young Jesuit with a number of obstacles. If these obstacles persist, and it becomes clear he does not seem equipped to persevere as a Jesuit, his superiors, after making a serene, objective evaluation of his difficulties, can have him freed from the commitment he made when he took his vows. However, these times of crisis are for the young companion first and foremost occasions to participate in brotherly conversation with those who have charge of enlightening his way and sharing his burden. The kind of obedience that is lived in the Society of Jesus makes this kind of conversation possible and relatively easy because it is an obedience that implies mutual confidence.[1]

For the man who perseveres, the ensuing years of studies in preparation for his priestly ordination and apostolate are often demanding and sometimes fraught with temptations.

Formerly, the different stages of this phase of training were more uniformly mapped out. Today, approaches to the humanities and literary studies are much more diversified. We have witnessed a

---

[1]See chapter 3, section 8, "Missionary Obedience."

multiplication of significant "languages," or modes of communication, in the world.[2] This has affected the formation of the apostle in the sense that choices must now be adapted to conform to individual needs; the training for each Jesuit must now be planned to fit the individual man.

This does not mean the formation "mold" of former times that sometimes enjoyed near-mythical reputation always served everyone in the exact same way. From the earliest days in the Society and throughout its history, there is evidence of how many Jesuits were involved in scientific or literary specializations, and how many eminent Jesuit scholars there were among men who had distinguished themselves in the different fields of science, humanities, and the arts.

To sum up, it is possible to say that today, as before, there are three stages which make up the curriculum proposed for the young Jesuits. These stages follow in sequence and are built around different clusters of courses. The first stage is a period of formation in the humanities—for example, in literature or the physical sciences; in mathematics or liberal arts, in history or law. The second stage is devoted to philosophy, and the third stage is dedicated to theology. The objective of this curriculum is to provide Jesuits with a technical mastery that is significant to his own culture, of paying attention to, and reflecting upon, the vital questions of the world of learning that concern human experience as a whole, and above all, in studying the Word of God, according to the tradition of the Church in order to become ministers of the priesthood of Jesus in today's world.

In the past, Jesuits have often been typified by the many years they spent in formation. Perhaps this still could be an apt characterization in a world where few priests go through the demands of a post-university training or study the sciences in depth. But the point here is that if Jesuits justifiably enjoyed such a reputation it is the Society of Jesus that deserves the credit. The Society has never been

---

[2][TRANSLATOR'S NOTE: The author uses the term "language" here and elsewhere in the sense that Pope Paul VI used it in *"Evangelii Nuntiandi,"* to which this present work is indebted. That is, "'language' should be understood . . . less in the semantic or literary sense than in the sense which one may call anthropological and cultural." *The Pope Speaks* (1976) 22:63. See also Pedro Arrupe, "On Inculturation," *Acta Romana Societatis Iesu* 17 *fasculus* 2 (1978), 277. "Language" here is therefore closer to the English term "communication skills."]

sparing when it comes to the formation of its members and it has always considered that studies seriously undertaken and pursued for as long a time as it takes to complete them are a satisfactory and sure investment.

Nevertheless, we recognize that holding fast to this policy today sometimes calls for more strongly tested conviction and greater courage than in the past. The temptation to take on instant-made pastoral ministries readily questions the worth of an intellectual and cultural preparation for the apostolate. Certainly this is a temptation we must resist. But we should also recognize something partially valid in this attitude. What is primarily being judged and condemned here is what is seen to be an ultra-theoretical or stilted type of formation, such as the kind which wormed its way into the plan of studies in less creative times.

The Thirty-second General Congregation (1974-75) considered the formation question and recommended a better integration of the three stages from the point of view of the apostolate, which is their purpose and their justification. But in this area a proper balance is not always easy to come by. How can anyone seriously doubt the positive character of any course that results in a genuine deepening of cultural understanding? After all, it is through language or communication skills that the universal and the concrete come together; and once the "show-me-the-instant result factor in activity begins to take over, the broadest vision is compromised, as well as the most fundamental understanding of problems.

Hence, the Society of Jesus' policy is to recognize the vital importance of "professional" philosophical and theological studies in the formation of the man, the religious, the priest and the apostle. St. Ignatius held that "studies demand the whole man," and he did not shy away from giving many detailed opinions in this matter even in the *Constitutions*. The Thirty-second General Congregation responded to Ignatius, as it were, when it stringently emphasized the essential unity between studies and the apostolate, both of which in some way have the same ultimate purpose.

Thus the Society has opted anew for a profound academic formation of its future priests—theological as well as philosophical, humane and scientific—in the persuasion that, presupposing the testimony of one's own life, there is no more apt way to exercise

our mission. Such study is itself an apostolic work which makes
us present to people to the degree that we come to know all the
more profoundly their possibilities, their needs, and their cultural
milieu. Our studies should foster and stimulate those very qualities which today are often suffocated by our contemporary style
of living and thinking: a spirit of reflection and an awareness of
the deeper, transcendent values. For this reason, our young men
should be reminded that their special mission and apostolate
during the time of study is to study. Thus, the desire for a more
active service, which the young feel so deeply, ought to be itself
the animating force which penetrates all their studies.[3]

The last general congregation likewise placed a new stress on
continuing formation. In a world of rapid change the ongoing process of updating is vital if one is to understand what men are saying
and what questions they are asking. It is also essential in order to
proclaim effectively the Word of God. Unless the apostle undergoes
a constant renewal, both in his spiritual and intellectual life, as well
as in his understanding of the here-and-now world where he lives, he
risks being on the wrong wavelength with the people he must serve.
Continuing formation means more than taking a formal approach to
a set store of knowledge, or of doing a kind of brushing up on
courses, or acquiring a determined number of facts. The important
element here is that the Jesuit be able to live and be at home—in the
most literal sense of that term—in the world as it is today; that he be
able to dialogue with the world and at the same time, irrespective of
all the socioeconomical cultural upheavals and dislocations of our
times, that he be a witness in the world to the Gospel.

§2. St. Ignatius of Loyola's Experience

At first sight, the policy of the Society of Jesus which calls for a long
period of time devoted to the pursuit of studies and for "cultural

---

[3]Sixth Decree, "The Formation of Jesuits, Especially with Regard to the Apostolate and
Studies," No. 22. In *Documents of the 31st and 32d General Congregations of the Society of
Jesus. An English Translation of the Official Latin Texts of the General Congregations and of
the Accompanying Papal Documents.* (St. Louis: Institute of Jesuit Sources), 450.

mediation" in its apostolic endeavors does not seem consistent with the road taken by Ignatius of Loyola after his conversion.[4]

As a matter of fact, culture did not appear to enjoy a high priority for Ignatius when, after being wounded at Pamplona he was converted to God and resolved to enroll himself in the school of the Lord; or afterwards either, when he put into execution his decision to make a pilgrimage to the Holy Land, where he had hoped both to find the living memory of Jesus the Savior in the holy places and to carry out a missionary task by preaching the Gospel to others, and where afterwards he saw himself offering his life to God in a noble-minded way. And is it not a fact that later when he went to Manresa, where he lived out his basic spiritual experience—from which the *Spiritual Exercises* came into being—he looked more like a vagabond than a "well-bred gentleman?" Moreover, did the first contact he had with God, his true "schoolmaster," leave him much room for cultural mediation? During this time of his life he became the butt of mocking children because he had decided not to pare his nails nor to cut his hair; to dress without the slightest care or the least concern about how he looked. If ever he condescended to, or even found, a need for having contact with his fellow human beings, it was not for the pleasure that cultural conversation brought but for the sole desire to share with others his discovery and experience of God. A short time afterwards, when he took the road for Venice intent on setting sail for Palestine, the poor "pilgrim," whose desire to rely on God alone for his daily fare sent him out on the streets to beg, was once again closer to being a "hippie" than a "well-bred gentleman."

---

[4][TRANSLATOR'S NOTE: The term "culture" throughout this book should be understood in the sense that this term is used in "The Proper Development of Culture" of the Vatican II Pastoral Constitution, *The Church in the Modern World* (53), *The Documents of Vatican II*, Walter M. Abbott, S.J., ed. (New York: Herder and Herder), 1966, 259-60. See also Paul VI, "Evangelii Nuntiandi," No. 20, *The Pope Speaks*, 21 (1976), 13; and in "Modern Catechetics: Message of the Faith Assembly of the Synod of Bishops to the People of God "(October 1977), No. 5 *The Pope Speaks* 23 (1978) 17. "Cultured mediation," a term used frequently in this study, implies a reciprocal exchange between the Gospel message and a given culture. The 1977 document "Modern Catechetics," issued by the Fifth Assembly of Synod of Bishops stated: "By means of catechesis the Christian faith must become incarnate in cultures. An authentic incarnation of the faith by means of catechesis supposes not only the process of "giving" but also the process of "receiving." *The Pope Speaks* 5 (1977) 17.]

It was his experience in Jerusalem that focussed his vision on a new need. Here his desire "to help souls," which he had already previously experienced, now became more and more pressing. From that moment on, Ignatius saw with greater clarity what he had to have in order to proceed along the way of apostolic service. That prerequisite he would acquire, thereby enabling him to ask the Church at a future date to accept him as one of her priests.

Ignatius was thirty-three when he returned to Europe. However, this advanced age was not an insurmountable obstacle for him. At Barcelona he set about studying grammar; at the universities of Alcalá, Salamanca, and Paris, he followed courses in the "arts" curriculum; that is, in philosophy and theology. This newly discovered need—to learn, to know, to train his intellect—drew its inspiration from the call he had heard, "to save souls." His unpleasant dealings with the Inquisition in Spain and to a lesser degree in Paris, only reinforced this conviction: If he wanted to become an apostle and a priest, he had to choose the required road to education. Even more, he had to give up everything that might present a hindrance to his studies during these years of preparation. He also came to see that learning about the prevailing culture of the day was a mandatory factor in the formation of the apostle and priest which he was called to be.

To be sure, Iñigo de Loyola would never become what might be termed a scholar. And Jesuits, then as now, are not, by virtue of their vocation, necessarily called to become specialists in some form or another of human learning. In the Society the ways of the apostolate are more diverse and more adapted to the resources and talents of each man. Nevertheless, what is basic to the spirit of Ignatius and will remain a conspicuously distinct feature of the religious order that he was called to found is the conviction that apostolic help offered to the neighbor demands intellectual preparation as well as spiritual formation. Furthermore, we may ask: Was it not from the academic setting, from his university friends, that Ignatius was able to find, one after another, qualified recruits for his apostolic project?

At the outset this project had a kind of vague shapelessness about it, and it was only progressively that it would lead him to found the Society of Jesus. However, from the very beginning and as a first step, he integrated a thoroughly priestly and apostolic training with school learning from renowned and esteemed academicians. We see the results in his first companions. Were not many of them selected to be theologians at the upcoming Council of Trent?

§3. The Apostolic View of Studies and Culture

Every Jesuit must confront the world of culture, and for the majority of Jesuits, this confrontation is not a cursory and superficial contact but a long and demanding road of specialization in one of the recognized branches of knowledge. However, the source of this demand is not found in an attachment to culture for its own sake; that is, the vocation to the Society of Jesus is not of itself a "vocation" to some form of humanistic studies. Were such the case, would it not present a peculiar kind of temptation to men whose religious vocation should otherwise separate them from the world and its illusions? The reason why the Jesuit is able to justify his need for scholarship, all ulterior partialities and attractions notwithstanding, is the same reason that led Ignatius, at thirty-three years of age, to take his place on a classroom bench—namely, the call to "help souls."

Since then, the same principle has governed the development of the Jesuit's formation and the dynamic apostolate of the Society. A willing acceptance of the world of culture in its most diversified forms comes from the premise that all things are in Christ. We stated above the purpose of the three stages in a Jesuit's formation is to train the young men in a knowledge of human languages, that is, in the systematic ways people today express ideas and feelings; to train them in philosophical reflections on these languages and on the questions they bring to the marketplace; and to imbue them with Jesus' Gospel in an effort to have them willingly contemplate God and to be totally committed to His Kingdom. The rest of this chapter will show how this threefold approach of the formation period leaves its indelible mark upon the companions and is reflected in their apostolic commitment.

It is because of their personal commitment that Jesuits can be found at work wherever culture is in the process of being formed or where it is being transmitted. They are involved in scientific, literary, or artistic research; they are even more active in the field of education. In the midst of these pursuits, however, their concern is to tie together human cultural aspirations with man's ultimate purpose in life. Indeed, it is in Christ, the Incarnate Word, that we receive the light that enables us to see a purpose in our history. The ways of expressing human ideas and feelings, the philosophical reflection on these activities, the acceptance of God's revelation—these are constantly linked together in the apostolic vision that motivates the Jesuit to follow the road of culture.

One example, perhaps the most impressive, can be given here to illustrate this point. On February 22, 1551, the people of Rome might have read this inscription over the door of a modest dwelling at the foot of the Capitoline Hill: "School: grammar, humanities, and Christian doctrine. Free." This was the beginning of the Roman College, founded by Ignatius of Loyola. By 1553, philosophy and theology had been added to the already existing courses, and, in 1554, Pope Paul IV accorded the Jesuits the right to issue academic diplomas, and so the Roman College became a real university. Thirty years later this institution was given the name Gregorian University in honor of Pope Gregory XIII, who had endowed it with a new building.

Today the classes of "grammar" and "humanities" are separated from those whose purpose it is to teach the sacred sciences. But the curriculum in this ecclesiastical university, which is what the Gregorian is, continues to offer courses parallel to philosophy and theology. These are not only courses in the "auxiliary sciences," that is, in subjects relating to Church-oriented studies, such as canon law, Church history, missiology, spirituality, and the like, but also courses in purely humanistic disciplines, including psychology and the social sciences.[5]

Jesuits, in developing the work of education in the Society of Jesus, certainly had to adapt themselves to the various exigencies of different times and places, while seeking for ways to bring together

---

[5]This university is especially known as having an *international* character both because of the faculty and student body. Today more than eighty nations are represented among approximately 2,500 students, about two-thirds of whom are either priests or seminarians. There are two institutions of higher ecclesiastical learning associated with the Gregorian University, both unique in their field of specialty and each under the direction of the Society of Jesus: The Pontifical Biblical Institute (center for biblical studies) and the Pontifical Oriental Institute (center for studies dealing with the Eastern Churches).

men of all countries in accord with their specific cultural expectations. But in the multiplication of colleges and universities, about which we shall treat below, there were always departments of philosophy and theology in such diverse places as France, Germany, Italy, Spain, Belgium, and Poland, as well as in the United States, Canada, Latin America, and Africa.

Where people talk, where they express themselves, where they converse with one another and profess their hopes, there they also tell about—often without knowing it—how they are waiting for God.

This is the world of all languages that at each historical moment Jesus asks to be united with; it is a multiform world, which the Word wants to teach, convert, and fulfill. This is the world of many languages into which Jesus sends apostles and companions, to announce His salvation, these are the languages they must endeavor to understand and, in some way, be at home with, so that in time the life-giving presence of the good news of revelation and salvation will take hold.

Let no one fear that such a description equates culture and human communication skills with a set of "instruments" employed for the purpose of spreading the Gospel! To do so would be to misread their specific human values. It would imply a very poor understanding of man and of the Gospel as well. It would be as if the bond which ties one to the other were somehow extrinsic to both; as though the fusing of the two were not based on what is totally human and "catholic," in the Christian sense of the term, and finally as if we paid no heed to the all-embracing philanthropy of God who made Himself visible to us in Jesus of Nazareth.

In the light of Jesus, Son of Man and Son of God, it is impossible for the Christian to represent the interrelationship between the human and the divine ways in a dualistic manner. However, the "unifying" vision, which is the Christian's vision, has nothing of the totalitarian about it that could stifle freedom. This unifying perception is rooted in God's covenant with man, an alliance engraved with complete respect for man's liberty. It is in Him, who is "the way, the truth and the life," and in whom has shone forth in a spectacular way the integral truth about man and God, that the human and divine ways now converge once and for all—the way God takes to come to our world, offering us His light and love, and the way on which we, now aware of our total freedom as men, are put enroute by Him, who is the "way," toward the Father of all goodness.

When a culture truly says something about man, it already shows forth the image of God, which God's creative love has imprinted in man, and it witnesses to the movement of the Spirit who, without always revealing His origin ("You cannot tell where He comes from or where He is going" John 3:8), comes forth and breathes life into man's quest for God. In the words used to express a culture, the Word of Truth is already there, as it were, stammering, striving to be expressed clearly, to be revealed. When we attempt to learn about any culture, we link up with the movement of the Spirit inscribed in the depths of every human mode of expression. The person who has his eyes focused contemplatively on Jesus, the living Word of God, can see sketched out in the expression of culture the place where His presence and His glory dwell.

We recognize both the difficulty and the terrible exigency of an undertaking such as we have briefly outlined here. It means entering into contact with all cultures, in order to find within them the already hidden, and often the blood-stained presence of Jesus, and it calls for helping cultures to go to the core of their inner vitality, at which point they can open themselves up to the truth of the Lord and of His message of revelation. This is an undertaking that comes about with much patience and often through many trials, but it is an effort spurred on by this certitude: For every living being and for all the *nations*, "Jesus Christ is the Lord."

The one who takes on such a commitment is spared neither traps nor failures. Indeed, cultures are the places where the totality of a history is voiced, a history not only with its expectations and searchings but also with its meanderings and countless detours. If the human heart is complex, if it is the battlefield of the for-or-against struggle with God, if it is the dwelling place for so many conflicting tendencies and desires which no one of us is prepared to see clearly within oneself, then what can be said of cultures, the hub where countless manipulative forces, all at variance with one another, crisscross and converge; the arena wherein so many men are forced to speak of their strengths as well as their weaknesses, of their darknesses as well as their lights? When Jesus came to live among His people, who had gone through a long period of preparation, was He not shut off by misunderstandings, obstacles, rejections? And was not His word a scandal for many? Afterwards, this word had to extract the necessary force and clarity from different traditions and in later times in order to be understood. What roads of conversion did we not force it to pass through!

The Jesuit finds himself totally immersed by the demands and exigencies of this problem because of the missionary calling alive within him, guiding him in his experience with culture. Every human language should affirm Jesus as Lord, but how can it say yes to name Him in praise, in thanksgiving and in adoration as the Lord?

During the Age of the Renaissance, when the Society of Jesus began its apostolic venture, it became apparent that the Christian purpose of culture had to be made known and broadcast. Today, when ideological disputes openly challenge the foundations of faith in God and the Christian vision of man and society, such a serious attempt is no less significant and no less urgent. In this area spiritual and pastoral discernment must go hand-in-hand with the ability to appreciate clearly the world of ideas in order to insure a successful outcome in the dialogue between the faith and different segments of our contemporary culture.

The foundations for the Christian understanding of the world of history can be laid out at the very earliest stages of education. However, it is essential that the superstructure of learning and the reflection which comes from the acquisition of knowledge continue to be constructed along the same lines. It is for this reason that we shall describe in this chapter, which deals with culture in general, the apostolate of Jesuit education and other forms of the cultural apostolate that the Society of Jesus lists among its undertakings.[6]

---

[6]The formation of the young Jesuit gives evidence of the Christian and apostolic end of culture which we have briefly described. Thus, during the time between his studying philosophy and theology, he is given some apostolic responsibility for a few years. This period constitutes a part of his formation. It is a time when he begins to see with greater clarity the missionary orientation of his studies. Moreover, as we have indicated above, the Thirty-second General Congregation decreed the need to integrate all Jesuit formation in the light of the apostolate.

§4. Jesuit Colleges

The reason the Society of Jesus has focussed its efforts on education stems from its purpose to be accessible to a variety of cultures and in turn to have access to them. Education is important to the inculturation process.

When a person consciously builds within himself a place for the encounter between the Gospel and human inquiries, between Jesus' revelation and the human quest for truth, he gradually becomes aware of his capacity for being a teacher. This skill is not limited to classroom instruction in its technical and formal sense; however, this does not mean that one has the right to be contemptuous of the sciences and humanities as disciplines. The educator's skill is the ability to demonstrate, through a willingness to learn, a respect for man, never shutting him off, esteeming every value he has discovered through which to express himself. The capacity for being a Jesuit teacher includes a recognition that such human values are a *praeparatio evangelica*. Even more, Jesuit humanism enables a person to see in these values the means for completing the process which makes man God's creature.

People have exalted or have condemned the humanism of the Jesuits. Some have been tempted to consider Jesuit high schools and universities as the apostolate par excellence of the Society of Jesus, even though education was only one form among others, however important, for providing the sustenance of the world with the leavening power of the Gospel.[7] It seems to me that we must see the teaching and educational work accomplished by the Jesuits as the normal outgrowth of a faith in man's ability to come to full stature in Jesus Christ. The key to this is the *Spiritual Exercises*.

The pedagogy which the colleges and universities of the Society of Jesus has sought to develop and which has made them successful is, as a matter of fact, inspired by the *Spiritual Exercises*. Consequently, it is a method of teaching that has an unlimited respect for man, for

---

[7][TRANSLATOR'S NOTE: The term *collège* in French corresponds to what is a combination American secondary school and junior college. All of the references that the author makes to the French *collège* could be compared to the American high school and university.]

his freedom and his culture, and at the same time it endeavors to open this freedom and culture to what is truly Christocentric. The Jesuit teacher seeks to beget in the other whatever he has already discovered in himself and, thanks to which, he is in harmony with God's speaking to him through a given culture. There are, of course, totalitarian cultures, but the Jesuit educator does not consider these because they represent a type of humanism drained of sense.

A history of the genesis of the first colleges of the Society of Jesus clearly shows that the way of educating the individual Jesuit dictated to some extent the Society's educational philosophy.

In the beginning, the colleges were merely the places of residence for young Jesuits during the period of their formation. Those in charge of the newborn Society recognized the need for a solid and serious formation in the areas of sciences and the humanities, as well as in philosophy and theology. Jesuit high schools and universities of today evolved from these pristine colleges. But before this process was able to begin, there were two policy decisions that Ignatius had to make. The first came about as a result of circumstances that had developed at the proposed College of Gandía, Spain, in 1546. Rather than having the Jesuit students, or scholastics as they are called, sent elsewhere to make their studies, St. Ignatius decided that they would be taught by Jesuit teachers there at the college itself. Founded on the basis of this policy decision, the College of Gandía was elevated to the status of a university the following year by Pope Paul III. The second action taken by Ignatius was even more eventful in the process we are attempting here to highlight. Why, it was asked, should a type of teaching whose value was discovered to have universal appeal be limited to members of the Society? Why reserve the transmission of a knowledge and culture to young Jesuit scholastics when it could for so many others be the point of mediation between humanism and a growth in Christ? The upshot was the decision to open up the colleges to the public, which marked the beginning of an extraordinary burgeoning of colleges operated by the Society of Jesus.

During the middle of the eighteenth century, fully two hundred years after its foundation, the Society counted 679 colleges under its care. The total number of educational institutions operated by the Jesuits is still today very high: There are 115 centers of higher education, 400 secondary schools, 150 technical schools and more than 200 primary schools.[8] The total number of students in all of these institutions is more than one million. However, the colleges in Europe are now less numerous than before: In Italy during the past two centuries they have declined from 133 to 8; in Germany and Austria from 101 to 6; in Poland from 44 to 0. On the other hand, during this same period their growth in North and South America, in Asia and in Africa has been impressive.

There are some fundamental principles that have always governed the educational undertakings of Jesuit high schools and universities: The quality of teaching, the attention given to every aspect of education and to a humane and Christian integration of the different branches of learning, and training of trustworthy men (and in more recent times, women) who have been able to give direction to their communities through the exercise of their chosen fields of expertise and by their participation in social organization.

However, because the Society of Jesus wants its educational work today to be focused on the human and spiritual welfare of the person and society, these fundamental principles beg for a renewed hearing. The Thirty-second General Congregation has clearly expressed the option for service of the faith and the promotion of justice.[9] In the words of the former superior general of the order, Father Pedro Arrupe, this option can be implemented in the area of Jesuit education by the formation of "agents for change." Student recruitment and curriculum planning are being programmed to take this particular need into consideration.

Of course, it is not possible to preach the Gospel openly in all Jesuit schools nor in every school where Jesuits make up part of the staff. Just imagine the huge number of Hindu, Muslim, or Buddhists who come to Jesuit institutions to be educated! This fact does not mean, however, that options based on spiritual principles should be conspicuous by their absence, for it is such principles that direct the vision of man and his social responsibilities.

---

[8]Today these figures are more approximate than exact. The evolution of a number of institutions does not allow them to be any longer considered specifically Jesuit. Today, policies of collaboration between Jesuits and lay people are manifold. (For more current statistics, see "Directory: Jesuit Educational Institutions," Rome: 1990.)

[9]See Chapter 3, section 9, "Service of the Faith and Promotion of Justice."

The companions of Jesus have always found educational centers, arenas where a relatively diversified population can gather. These places are hubs of vital contact, where dynamic forces in society and culture intersect, where the conveying of our traditional forms of knowledge opens out to the new hopes of the future. There the Jesuits deal not only with children or with the young who come to them to be taught but also with the parents of these young people and other mature individuals, already involved in their careers, who are looking for the encouragement and support they need in order to carry out their responsibilities with more assurance. The place for such meetings may be a church or a cultural center, often adjacent to the school itself. Being in close proximity to where other Jesuits carry on their apostolate explains why the center is where it is. At the same it offers the Jesuits in the school or parish opportunities to broaden their influence among people who work in the downtown section or live in the nearby neighborhoods.

Jesuits do not work alone in their various educational enterprises, and less so today than ever before. The Second Vatican Council cast a more intense light on the role of the laity in the Church. And the lay people who collaborate in the educational work of the Society of Jesus are, with good reason and in the most responsible way, part of the dedicated service provided by Jesuit high schools and universities. At the present time these lay people work side-by-side with the religious of the Society at every level of organization, administration and direction in Jesuit educational institutions. They bring their particular gifts and talents to instruction and education, whose source of inspiration, as we have already pointed out, is the vision of man and history outlined by St. Ignatius for us in his *Spiritual Exercises*. It is a vision totally centered on the mystery of Christ, on Him who has revealed God to us and given us the final word on humanity itself.

§5. Other Forms of the Cultural Apostolate

In order to be brief, we have, in the preceding section, spoken almost exclusively about Jesuit high schools, colleges, and universities. But what we have said about the Jesuit philosophy of education is applicable elsewhere. The secular university also is a place for preaching the Gospel through cultural mediation.[10] Furthermore, literacy programs as well as adult education classes, so necessary and urgent for the future welfare of the so-called undeveloped nations, are likewise an apostolate characterized by the same imperative and the same spirit. Here again, it is the Society's policy to pay attention to the needs of any people it means to serve in the name of the Gospel.

But education is not limited to classroom teaching. It should be undertaken in every available way and for people of all age groups, wherever possible. The culture of a people expresses itself as an extension of their daily lives. It invades their personal lives more than ever in a civilization where the working hours are limited and where the technology offers more leisure and more occasions to participate in community activities.

The same drive which once led Jesuits to found colleges now imposes upon them the imperative to be present wherever modern man's opinions and feelings are being forged, recast, and voiced aloud. More than at any other time Jesuits today should become involved with groups of professionally qualified laypeople so that they can adapt their apostolate to the culture of the men and women whom they are trying to reach.

Today there are Jesuits working in university laboratories, astronomical observatories, and research centers. They are there because that is where the development of human knowledge and science, so vitally important for an appreciation of peoples and societies, is taking place. Jesuits also edit multi-language periodicals throughout the world. They do so because they want to communicate the message of salvation to their brothers and sisters with whom they collaborate in research projects or in discussing important issues of the day. These magazines and journals are geared to different types of readers. Some are highly scientific and therefore intended for

---

[10][TRANSLATOR'S NOTE: The Thirty-second General Congregation decreed that "Wherever we serve we must be attentive to "inculturation"; that is, we must take pains to adapt our preaching of the Gospel to the culture of the place so that men and women may receive Christ according to the distinctive character of each country, class or group and environment." *Documents of the 31st and 32d General Congregations of the Society of Jesus*, [85], 242. The term "cultural mediation" therefore refers to adapting the Gospel message to the cultural environment of the people to whom the Jesuit has been sent.]

special groups of scholars and specialists in a particular field of knowledge; then there are magazines of "more general interest," where the news of the day is looked at according to different points of view and then analyzed according to true humane and Christian values; there are also reviews which are theological, philosophical, scientific or literary in scope.[11]

Thanks to the ready availability of mass education, our world today has witnessed a cultural revolution. In an effort to describe this new cultural environment in which we are living, we sometimes speak of it as an audio-visual-centered culture, referring to the influence of the latest modes of communication. Audio-visual media are endowed with the power of forming opinions and the ability to influence an ever-expanding number of people. This is a new phenomenon, the importance of which has scarcely been overestimated.

As a result of this media revolution, a certain form of pan-globalism has become possible at the cultural level. It is easier today than ever before to be informed not only about what is happening in our own communities but also about what is happening in other parts of the globe. But if this opening up to the distant and different is to remain more than academic, then it is necessary that this information engender a much broader based policy of involvement and collective responsibility.

What has to come about and develop through the media— newspapers, radio, television—is a new moral awareness of human and social realities and a new resolve to do as much as possible to deal with the most critical problems threatening mankind's existence and its culture. But we will not live through this revolution in an honest way unless we are resolved to respect, and search for, truth. This way we will do our utmost to make progress in liberty and love, not relying on partisan ideologies, deceptions, or disguises that con-

---

[11]The following is a representative listing of American Jesuit periodicals published in English: *America, Blueprint for Social Justice, Company, Human Development, New Testament Abstracts, Review for Religious, Studies in the Spirituality of the Jesuits, Theological Studies, Theology Digest* and *Thought.* Two Braille publications are *Deaf and Blind Weekly* and *The Catholic Review.* There are also a number of distinguished publishing houses: Georgetown University Press (Washington, D.C.), The Institute of Jesuit Sources (St. Louis), Loyola University Press (Chicago), and Ignatius Press (San Francisco), which also publishes the English edition of the magazine *130 Days.*

ceal the truth or distort reality. Jesuits, insofar as their limited resources permit, want to be counted among those who take part in this
movement which is so crucial to the future of human society.[12]

Jesuits also give equal attention to other types of communication
that are unquestionably more modest, but which, thanks to the image
and impressions they evoke, have more easily become instruments
for evangelization. We cannot overlook teaching Jesus' message with
the help of pictures and with new and various show-and-tell techniques for bringing the truths of the faith to the people. In Latin
America, particularly, Jesuits use the radio to catechize. They do so
in cooperation with more than a dozen national educational agencies.
Moreover, they have also developed the use of cassettes, slides, and
pamphlets there to stimulate the work of reflection on the Gospel
message in what are called "base communities."

However, it would be illusory—in this area more than anywhere
else—to take refuge in a kind of triumphalism. The means of communication which have the greatest lasting effects on human groups
are very often beyond any possible influence on the part of the
Church. In many places any cleric appearing in his role as priest
would not be the most influential and suitable channel for making
the Lord's Gospel palatable. This is so even if he limits himself to
commenting on those parts of the Gospel which enjoin all to have a
respect for man and his dignity, and call for building up human
societies in a peaceful, tranquil way. Humbly, patiently, and ac-
knowledging their limits and shortcomings, as well as their foot-
dragging in adjusting and being open to what is new, Jesuits do not
want to exclude using any instrument which holds out to the modern
world the possibility, through the most diverse human, social, and
cultural resources, of becoming a witness to God and His Christ.
Jesus has taken on, in Himself, all that is human. This same exigency
and urgency ever consumes the hearts of Jesuits and sustains the
enthusiasm of their faith because no human means of expression is
indifferent to this mystery of the Incarnation. This is why the reality

---

[12]We should point out here that ever since the foundation of the Vatican Radio some
fifty years ago, the popes have graciously entrusted the Jesuits with its direction. Today
there are about thirty of them who work in the administrative offices and on programs
offered in several of different languages.

of this mystery and its glory consist in embracing and transfiguring everything that each and every one of Jesus' brothers experiences. It also consists, insofar as it is possible to do so, in making this mystery understood and appreciated by all men so as to fulfill a not always conscious anticipation whose presence risks being stifled by comfort-loving practices. Such practices are readily available in a number of continents and among different social classes.

Living in a world that experiences a dearth of values, that despairs, and that goes after tinsel paradises, today's Companion of Jesus feels keenly the price that both individuals and societies must pay when they forget what it is that makes them live and when they equate happiness with shallow, instant gratification that can never really satisfy the human heart.

To be a witness to Christ in the midst of human cultures is to wait for love and its fulfillment in God. God brings pressure to bear on human societies, without their knowing it and sometimes even in spite of what they themselves try to promote, and He acts through all the endeavors of these societies to help them realize their authenticity and to express the inner riches that dwell within them.

§6.   Two Examples of Inculturation

From the earliest days of its history, the Society of Jesus, which is essentially a missionary order, has watched a good number of her sons depart for foreign countries. No one needs to be reminded of the name Francis Xavier, for example. And how many other Jesuits since his day have been rushed headlong into the adventure of missions in far-off lands! Jesus taught that the Good News be brought to all nations; therefore, it is not necessary to search further for the motivation that animated these men to spread the Word, especially during a period when nations of the West had set sail to explore the world. It is easy today to harbor suspicions about their ventures, which were often enough mixed up with the mishaps of western colonialism. In doing so, however, we would not only risk overlooking all the sufferings and the self-denial of the Society's first generation of missionaries but we would also fail to recognize how much these men had given up to leave the familiarity of their native lands and to become newcomers, for better or worse, in distant, mysterious civilizations, whose languages and customs were totally foreign to them.

These early Jesuit missionaries implemented a basic way of acting which can be appreciated only in the light of Christ's relationship to the different cultures where His message is to be preached. The choice they made, in fact, had already been made by the apostles at the beginning of the Church's history, at its first council, the Council of Jerusalem. At that time the question was: Should they allow pagans to be baptized without first initiating them into the observances of the Mosaic Law? The apostles decided that, without compromising the unique role of Israel, the people of the Covenant and of the messianic expectation out of which Jesus, the Son of God, was born, the Church had to adapt Christ's message to the Gentile culture. Such a decision implied an attitude of continual openness and adaptation on the part of missionaries to the culture where they were preaching Christ.

Jesuits are sensitive to the demands of a personal insertion into the culture of the region where their apostolate is carried on, and, even if they have not always been enthusiastic in implementing this process of integration, cultural mediation does goes go hand-in-hand with their spirituality in a very special way. In connection with this point we would like to present to the reader the names of two pioneers of what we call today "inculturation." We do not introduce these resolute, courageous forefathers of ours because we want to pat ourselves on the back, but rather because they witness to the resourcefulness that still today embodies the spirituality of the Society of Jesus and its way of preaching the Gospel. Nobili and Ricci are names that epitomize how the companions of Jesus take on the identity of people to whom they have been sent to preach salvation.

India was the field for the apostolate of Robert de Nobili (1577-1656). The difficulties he encountered there in his attempt to make the leaven of the Gospel penetrate Hindu society led him to adopt the practices of the highest Indian castes. He became a Brahman among Brahmans, embraced their way of ascetical life, and carried on a fruitful dialogue with them, in which not only the subject and successes of science were discussed, but also the novelty and truth of Christianity. At the same time, some of his other companions, likewise endowed with the same openness and the same spirit of unselfish adaptation, lived among the pariahs and the lower castes of Indian society.

Matteo Ricci (1552-1610) used his scientific knowledge in order to make contact with the Mandarin scholars of China to such an extent that he was soon recognized as being one of their peers and, as an astronomer and mathematician, he was received into the emperor's service. This was the result of fifteen years of continual efforts. But the way was now open and, with Adam Schall (1591-1666) and Ferdinand Verbiest (1626-1688), the Church in China was able to progress and become known to every class of people, from the lowly to the nobles of the Imperial Court.

The impact of the way chosen by Nobili, Ricci, and many others manifested itself during the quarrels known as the "Rites Controversy," which soon created a stir and put on trial this method of preaching the Gospel and implanting the Church in a foreign culture. In India as in China, Jesuit missionary policy had sought to integrate social and religious customs as much as possible into the practice of Christianity, and most visibly into the liturgy. But not everyone in the Church was convinced their methods were correct. Different religious orders were opposed to the Jesuits in the Rites Question and official complaints were sent on to Rome. In no time restrictions against this form of incarnating the Gospel message were issued, and then during the years that followed one pope would rescind these restrictions only to have his successor reconfirm them. At last, in 1742 the so-called "Chinese Rites" were condemned. A similar order was handed down to the Church in India in 1744. The debate lasted nearly a century, a proof of the complexity of the controversy. At that period of history the message of Christ was endeavoring to incarnate itself through Asian manners, customs, attitudes, and behaviors, but the ultimate solution forbade missionaries from making use of these modes of expression in preaching the Gospel.

Whatever were the subtleties of the entangled arguments and whatever were the obvious risks which had to be taken to open Christianity to new civilizations, the basic choice made by the early Jesuit missionaries was of an importance difficult to overestimate as far as the future of the Church and an understanding of its missionary work is concerned.

If Nobili, Ricci, and so many other Jesuits were the pioneers in this effort of inculturation, it is due no doubt to the cultural sensibility that a form of humanism rooted in the anthropology of the Spiritual Exercises had awakened in them. And, indeed, it was because of this sensitivity to other cultures that they discovered a freedom in their approach to, and an outspokenness in, their dialogue with a world which was almost totally new to them. The question boils down to this: How to plant the Gospel into the rich soil of any one culture without attempting to equate it with some other historical and cultural pattern? Jesus became enfleshed, He appeared in a particular culture and He expressed Himself in a particular language. But He did not for that reason wish to limit His word and His revelation to those men and women of that culture or to those who spoke that specific language. Rather he wanted to bring to fulfillment the expectation of a messiah for all people and all cultures, the hope that was already inscribed within the revelation to Israel of His universal message. Lord of history, Christ still wishes today to encounter, historically and culturally, all those whom the Father has given to Him to become His brothers and sisters. He still desires to bring into the same unique vine—that is into the Church, where the life which comes from the Father and which conforms to Christ's filial vocation circulates—those who at all times and in all places are prepared to accept the divine meaning of their destiny so as to be able to respond to it.

§7. The Challenge of Inculturation

On May 14, 1978, Father Pedro Arrupe, at that time the general of the Society of Jesus, addressed a letter to all the members of the order on the subject of inculturation. In this letter he responded to a mandate issued by the Thirty-second General Congregation.[13]

He noted that the fundamental principle of inculturation "is that [it] is the incarnation of Christian life and of the Christian message in a particular cultural context, in such a way that this experience not

---

[13][TRANSLATOR'S NOTE: The congregation decreed that it "entrusts to Father General the further development and promotion of this work throughout the Society. In the first place it recommends that, after he has considered the whole question with the help of expert assistance, Father General write a letter of instruction to the entire Society, in order to further this work in and by the Society. His purpose in writing will be to clarify for all of Ours the true meaning and theological understanding of the task and process of inculturation as well as its importance for the apostolic mission of the Society today." Decree 5: "The work of Inculturation of the Faith and Promotion of Christian Life," of "The Society's Response to the Challenges of our Age." In *Documents of the 31st and 32d General Congregations of the Society of Jesus*, 439-40. Father Jerome Aixalá observed that "Inculturation—at least the term—was born in the (Thirty-second General) Congregation. Pedro Arrupe, "On Inculturation," *Selected Writings*, 3:171.]

only finds expression through elements proper to the culture in question (this alone would be no more than a superficial adaptation) but becomes a principle that animates, directs, and unifies the culture, transforming and remaking it so as to bring about 'a new creation.'"[14]

To a certain degree the movement here is twofold. The Christian message takes shape in each culture, and at the same time, the culture spurs it on to yet uncharted possibilities. Then the culture is drawn away from the world, which is so hedged by the barrier of its own idols that it cannot find, in the liberty of the Spirit, the breath which shapes and creates it anew.

The question here should not be posed only in regard to cultures of those places which we have referred to up until now as "mission lands." If in the course of World War II, André Godin (1906-1944) could understandably write a pastoral reflection on whether France, deputed to be a Catholic country, was not in fact missionary territory, then today, surely, the law of inculturation that accompanies the work of evangelization is necessarily even broader and more universal: It is concerned with all cultures and subcultures of our day, with all continents and with all countries. It shows in what way we should strive to make the Christian message accessible and really challenging for all peoples.[15] Such an effort is not accomplished in one day, but it is to be taken up relentlessly again and again. It calls for a continuous pastoral dialogue with the prevailing culture in the light of the mystery of Jesus.

For this reason Jesuits were invited by their superior general not to refuse "the effort of creativity" which today involves "the evangelization of cultures." And Father Arrupe, by addressing the Society of Jesus and by citing the authority of its spirituality and tradition, was eager to repeat this point asserted by Pope Paul VI in his 1975 apostolic exhortation *Evangelii nuntiandi* (on proclaiming the Gospel).[16]

A working paper accompanied Father Arrupe's letter to the members of the Society of Jesus. This document began with a series

---

[14]Pedro Arrupe, "On Inculturation," *Selected Writings*, 3:173.

[15]André Godin, *France Pagan? The Mission of Abbé Godin.* Translated by Maisie Ward. (New York: Sheed and Ward, 1959).

[16]Pedro Arrupe, "A Working Paper on Inculturation: Preliminaries," *Acta Romana Societatis Iesu*, 17, *fasciculus* 2 (1978), 266-67.

of "preliminaries," which specified in detail the concept of inculturation, emphasized its need and its historic importance, and finally, listed the groups who are carrying it out and the variety of approaches they might make in doing so.

Inculturation is understood as "the effort that the Church makes to present the message and values of the Gospel by embodying them in expressions that are proper to each culture, in such a way that the faith and Christian experience of each local church is embedded, as intimately and deeply as possible, in its own cultural context.[17]

Perceiving "more clearly than ever before the urgency" of putting an end to the "unsatisfactory relationship of the content of the Gospel message" to the terms it employs, and of the forms of faith to the Christian life itself, the Church has been encouraged to discover "fresh treasures in the inexhaustible source of Revelation," in the fulfillment of her function to preach the Gospel in an age of transition like our own.[18]

The task to be achieved is not easy because the Gospel message and the expression of Christian faith and life "touches what is deepest and most sensitive in the human heart."[19]

In such a work there has to be a cooperative effort from the hierarchy, the theologians, the specialists in human sciences, and, just as important, from the people of God "with their traditions, their ancestral wisdom, their intuitions, their sensibilities and apprehensions, which have developed certain forms of expression over the centuries." And this work of inculturation should not be limited to different "ethnic groups"; it ought to pay attention also to the "various cultural levels that cut across established geographical boundaries," such as, the scientific world, for example.[20]

The movement that brings about this work in multiple ways can only put forward "distinct aspects of the same Spirit who wants all men to listen to the Word of God and draw their life-blood from it."[21]

---

[17]Ibid., 266.

[18]Ibid.

[19]Ibid.

[20]Ibid., 267.

[21]Ibid.

III

Apostolic Service

§1. "Serve as a Soldier under the Standard of the Cross"

The expression "Serve as a soldier under the standard of the cross" has a military ring to it. Does this mean then that the Companion of Jesus is expected to enlist in an army? And does the standard under which he fights symbolize some ideal of conquest or reconquest? Some people might be inclined to imagine the onetime knight in armor, which Iñigo de Loyola was, transposing his former military ésprit de corps into the religious life.

But it need not be understood that way. Iñigo was really converted and his conversion resulted in a change not only of his goal but also of his method and vision. Even in those places where he continues to make obvious use of military images, we should see that what he is doing is pointing out oppositions and contrasts to worldly ideals, including those of service.

Such is the case, for example, in two key meditations of the *Spiritual Exercises*. In order to awaken and sustain the desire to serve Christ the Lord, Ignatius proposes that the retreatant first of all imagine "the call of an earthly king," and to fancy the enthusiasm that such a call would conjure up were the king to invite his subjects to join with him in a plan of *reconquista*.

However, the atmosphere changes when the person is asked to visualize Christ our Lord. First of all, the project of joining forces with a leader is no longer the only concern, nor is the enterprise which is to be undertaken. Rather, what is of primary importance is the sharing in a common life: I am invited to live my life with Christ in suffering, and later in glory. The fact is that the extraordinary invitation on the part of this "Eternal King," addressed to me personally, makes me want to become like Him so that I in turn may find joy in sharing His life.

Clearly, the promise to be in Jesus' company is no different from the one proposed in the Gospel: It means leaving all in order to follow Him, which, for me, consists in stripping myself of what I desire in order to give myself entirely to His work, expecting every day to find in Him, and to receive from Him, life's sustenance

Hence, it is primarily in myself that the converting and conquering action takes place. This same point is highlighted in a most striking way in the second key meditation of the *Spiritual Exercises* to which we referred above.

Here the question is a choice between two options, between two standards, corresponding to two opposing declarations of principles, modeled after St. Augustine's two cities. On the one hand, we have the standard of him whom St. Ignatius describes as "the deadly enemy of our human nature." He looks for subterfuges to draw people into slavery by using such powerful levers as the desire to covet riches, the pursuit of empty honors, and the will of overweening pride. To enlist under this standard ultimately leads to the loss of liberty because the person fails to recognize the essential nature of freedom, which is to be rid of one's ego in order to find, as the reward, one's true fulfillment. The second standard is that of the true Lord of the universe. Far from wanting to subject the person who enlists under this standard, Christ's humility and gentleness seek to awaken in him the desire for truth and authentic liberty, which often lie dormant in the depths of the human heart. The road He proposes that one take seems difficult, but no one can find peace apart from it. It is through poverty rather than through wealth that Jesus promises liberty and joy, through insults or contempt, rather than through the honor of this world, and through humility of heart before God, rather than through the rash pride that leads man to go even so far as to substitute himself for his Master and Lord.

It is the heart of man himself that must be conquered. Such an operation puts the greatest demands on him, leaving him little place for cravings of a military nature, for dreams of power, or for the ideals of the belted knight as they are lived out in the logic of this world. In one sense it is the complete reversal of life's logic because it implies the same logic St. Paul spoke about in the First Letter to the Corinthians, where he contrasts pagan wisdom to the folly of the cross, and greedy power which stands out in external show to the weakness of God manifested in Jesus![1]

Such is the "standard of the cross," under which the Jesuit is called to "go serve as a soldier."[2] Self-conquest is the gauge for measuring the authenticity of all that he will do in the service of the Kingdom. It is within this context that we should go back to the solemn declaration from the General Examen that is given to candidates seeking entrance into the Society of Jesus:

> The end of this Society is to devote itself with God's grace not only to the salvation and perfection of the members' own souls but also with that same grace to labor strenuously in giving aid toward the salvation and perfection of the souls of their fellowmen.[3]

Just as it was for Ignatius, apostolic service in the life of a Jesuit is inseparable from the work of self-reform, of renewing his own heart, of becoming conformed to Christ Jesus. This christoforming activity in turn engenders and fosters within the companion the inescapable demand for an apostolate where he will not spare his energies, but where he can devote himself courageously and generously to the labor of Him who is for all the one and only Savior.

The account in the tenth chapter of St. Matthew's Gospel, where we read about the apostles being sent out on mission was a particularly inspiring passage for Ignatius, and so should it be for his disciples. It is a narrative which should serve to mobilize all their forces. In this account Jesus is the one who sends His apostles; it is in His name that each must be ready to journey throughout the world, provided with this one certainty: the Kingdom is in our midst; the seed needs but to grow; we are at the starting point of a new humanity reconciled to itself and to God. The adversities along the road are not important, nor are misunderstandings and even persecutions the apostle may encounter, as long as he is conscious that he lives for this thirst to

---

[1] 1 Corinthians 1:22-25.

[2] "Whoever desires to serve as a soldier [*militari*] of God beneath the banner of the cross in the Society, which we desire to be designated by the name of Jesus . . . " "Formula of the Institute," *Constitutions* [3], 66.

[3] "General Examen," *Constitutions* [3], 77.

communicate to his brothers and sisters the truth which he knows and loves; that is, the presence of the kind and compassionate God in their midst. In order to convey this message to them, he is ready, as was Christ before him, to deliver himself up, seeking nothing for himself, forgetting himself, and being able to live a truly poor life because he possesses deep within himself wonderful riches, which expand and increase by being shared with all, offered humbly to all.

For Jesuits "to serve as a soldier of God beneath the banner of the cross" means that they must constantly renew within themselves the depths of love, which the cross of Jesus reveals is limitless and unbounded; it means that they must beg for this love by striving to love; it means they must put into their own words—or to allow their own words gently or violently to be penetrated by—the imperious and magnetic power of the Word of wisdom, whose first and unique interpreter, Jesus, became every man in the eyes of his brothers and sisters. Sometimes it also means to have a dream, not a dream that pulls one away from reality but, to the contrary, a dream that throws one back to the real world with greater zeal and love for a new humanity that conforms to God's creative plan, penetrated by love and opening itself to love.

In a sense, this "army" or this service—which for the Companion of Jesus becomes ever more the reason for his life, the source of his joys and sadnesses, the place for his communion with God and with his brothers—this service cannot be chosen as one chooses a project, an activity to do, a work to be accomplished. Rather he allows himself to be empowered with it through the One who was sent by God for our salvation. This sending forth which confers on him his mission is the same sending forth of Jesus by His Father, a sending forth which continues down through the centuries: "As the Father sent me, so am I sending you."[4] This means that through my poverty and my sufferings I can be the witness for all to see Jesus carrying on His work today. Is not this worth the surrender of myself, the confidence that goes beyond what can be seen and tested, the serene enthusiasm of faith! Yes, God does watch over men. He sent His Son to save us and to open our eyes to the light. May these actions which spring from His paternal heart, create today in me, His child, a

---

[4]John 20:21.

driving force to continue the work of Jesus. There is no other solid base to look for upon which I can build my life, no other truth that can unseal my lips in offering thanks, than that of giving witness to the Word of freedom and salvation.

§2.   Sent in the Name of the Lord

If one has been sent in the manner of Christ, in the footsteps of Christ, in order to carry on the work of Christ, then it follows that he would have the inner resources to qualify him for the life of an apostle. The actual "sending" of such a man to a particular mission is simply a further necessary qualification to what he already is. In other words, he is a missionary prior to, and independent of, the particular mission to which he is, or will be, assigned.

It is enough to read the *Constitutions of the Society of Jesus* to discover the key factor that gives significance to the mission concept as a whole and to each of its parts as well. As early as April 22, 1541, when the first Companions of Jesus pronounced their vows in the Roman basilica of St. Paul-outside-the-Walls, they promised "to obey in everything in regard to the missions." And the same phrase is still repeated in the vow formula today as it was at the beginning of the Society: This binds the determination of the mission (whose source springs from trinitarian love, from the mystery of the Incarnate Word, and from the sending of the Holy Spirit who animates the Church) to the sovereign pontiff, the vicar of Christ on earth, or, in his place and position, to the superior general of the Society and to other superiors.

To be sent in this way is to realize in the deepest part of oneself that the means for carrying out the mission, doing what has to be done, completing the project, are not the products of the individual will, nor of any personal preference, however much these may be inspired by the will to do good.

The Jesuit who lives his life in missionary obedience has no other guiding principle for his ministry than the prevailing love of the Father who sends the Son and the Spirit to carry on Their work of revelation and sanctification. If it is through his sentiments, words, attitudes, actions, that this divine work is continued, the Jesuit also realizes that his being sent, which demands that he put himself at the disposal of the Church, is communicated to him by his superiors, and he knows that their word alone, expressed in God's name, concretely establishes and determines his missionary life and his missionary activity.

Every man likes to know that he is useful. It pleases him to take on a project that is not merely designed to suit his own particular interests or to guarantee his own self-fulfillment, because he finds joy in a self-effacement that serves some good to be accomplished, the joy in being able to give himself, to offer himself to an undertaking that transcends his own personal interests; in acting this way, his heart mobilizes interior and exterior resources and places them at his disposition. In this very activity he is able to find more self-fulfillment, a much greater peace, and a much greater joy than he could ever find in seeking self.

However, this law of unselfish giving is not by itself enough to define what is meant by "mission." As a matter of fact, it leaves in the shadow an essential dimension of missionary life. I should not only divest myself of all self-seeking in order to attain the end-result of the project to which I have been consigned. This self-effacement must be even more radical. It must be present when I make the initial choice to take on a specific work, at that moment when I am aware that I have made the choice to accept the assignment.

One must have experienced all of this in the context of one's faith in Christ, the unique Savior, and in His Word. From this point on my faith is the sole factor enabling me to see, in view of His work, how great an expansion of freedom comes from such a stance, which is a sure source of liberation. Obviously, such self-sacrifice cannot be lived honestly if the only reason for the choice is personal, any more, for example, than a person could authentically live a life of self-sacrifice in marriage if his motivation were primarily selfish. There would be a living contradiction in choosing not to choose anymore. But, if the call of Christ has been, and remains for me, the word at the very heart of my vocation that challenges me and restores me to myself, just as it did the disciples, then right from the very beginning I no longer find myself relying on my own initiative. I have not chosen, but I have been chosen; and the renunciation which expresses itself in the choice no longer to choose, is now but voicing the obverse side of the divine choice, which I must continue to receive in order to be authentically myself, to be able to understand myself just as I exist, and to be able to see myself from God's perspective and in His love's movement toward me: loved by Him so that I may serve, so that I may carry on His service for men, so that I may employ myself totally in what He gives me.

And there is nothing so much as the mystery of the Trinity which helps me understand why and how in living this way I partake in the life of the Son and become capable of being free as He was free.

Who was ever more free than Jesus? What man has known as He knew the completeness of a freedom that specifies itself only in terms of the ability to love, of being in the service of love? But when Jesus speaks of His mission, of His word, of His work, He clearly indicates the attitude of complete self-renunciation, beginning with that alone which He can, as Son, appropriate to Himself. This mission, this word, this work are not His, but they are confided to Him by His Father. To live a "missionary," an "apostolic" life is to be placed, by pure grace, in the very core of the experience that was lived by Jesus.

After the multiplication of the loaves, the Jews asked the Lord: "What must we do to carry out God's work?" In asking such a question, a man expresses the capacity of giving, offering, emptying out of self for God who receives His liberty. But Jesus' answer returns to this other self-effacement, where the secret of the missionary's life is expressed: "This is carrying out God's work: you must believe in the one He has sent."[5] The source therefore of the work to be carried out, its author, its subject, is something that goes beyond ourselves; it is God. But how does this come about if not in His Son, whom He sends among us in order to accomplish His work? How can He accomplish it if not through our faith, which makes us disposed to do the work of His Son in such a way that, for our part, we are able to continue His mission, being ourselves those who are sent?

The grace of the vocation, with which we have begun our reflection on the "way of the Society of Jesus," is inseparable from the grace of mission. If Jesus calls a companion it is to send him; and the response to the call is identified with the readiness to be sent. Thus it was in times past with the apostles: He "summoned those He wanted. So they came to Him and He appointed twelve; they were to be His companions and to be sent out to proclaim the message. . . "[6]

---

[5]John 6:28-29.
[6]Mark 3:13-14.

For Jesus' companion this experience is the source of the most profound joy and the most complete peace, even though it can carry with it enormous sacrifices and terrible sufferings. And even though he has already given his life to God, this experience must prevail over an array of different feelings that can trouble the serenity of his life.

It could be a man might feel himself more drawn to dedicate his energies to a work other than the one he has been given, or it might even be that, faced with an assignment, a man will experience fear draining all the courage he can muster. For instance, perhaps the inconvenience of picking up and moving some place else, of changing one's work, or leaving one's country might be the cause of distress. A man in such distress might be tempted to think, "I have given everything I have to the job I was doing; I was attached to people to whom the Lord had sent me and confided to my care. I felt the 'easy yoke'[7] of an apostolic office lived out in a love for the Lord and His brothers. And now He no longer wants me to carry on the work that once was mine; His voice calls me to go elsewhere, to weave new nets, to assume different responsibilities." Yet that man might better reason, "If, under such circumstances, something other than a fervent 'yes' offered to Christ resonates within my heart, I should ask myself if I had not been substituting myself for Him, the only Savior; if, all the while I had been giving myself so generously, I had not in fact been building a little kingdom of my own, and if, in seeking myself, I had not ended up finding only myself."

The demands of being accessible, however, do not manifest themselves only through the express order of a superior. The Jesuit himself can take the initiative by examining himself to see if he has the required qualities to take on a new assignment or to move on to a new place.

After World War II, when the general of the Society made an appeal to Jesuits from a number of provinces for volunteers for the Japanese Mission, he received a generous response from the whole order. This same scenario is repeated many times over right up to the present day. It is the same whether it takes the form of volunteering to be sent to Latin America or Africa, or going to offer modest help to groups of Asian or African refugees.

---

[7]Matthew 11:30.

Experiences are certainly very different in the area of apostolic availability. In fact, everyone who is sent to a mission writes a tale which is totally personal: the story of the companion. But beyond this diversity there is the same mystery that unfolds itself and before which the Jesuit finds himself "the useless servant." He must however "have done all"[8] wherever God has sent him so that his fidelity was proved and tested, and so that love was able to grow in his heart, gradually remaking him "to the image of the Son."[9]

§3. A Band of "Reformed Priests"

We have no way of knowing at what precise moment Ignatius decided that the Lord was calling him to be a priest. However, the studies he undertook after his return from Jerusalem, first in Spain and later at Paris, were in fact studies required for ordination to the priesthood.

Ignatius was by no means blind to the scandals involving the Church and the priests of his time. He, who refrained from judging the Church and had no other desire but to serve her, also knew the demands of the Gospel and the demands implied in the conversion of one's life. The priesthood cannot express the total gift of Jesus to His own "so that they may have life and have it to the full" in any meaningful way unless the priest renounces the pursuit of honors, social promotions, and financial interests.[10] To receive the priesthood of Jesus, as a ministry to be exercised for the good of the Church, means being called to espouse His sentiments, which are the sentiments of "emptying out" and of even "accepting death." Indeed it is here that the "Lordship" of Jesus manifests the "glory of God" and that His "name" receives the praise the Father has bestowed upon it.[11]

As soon as they were ordained, the first Companions of Jesus began to exercise their ministry in this spirit of humility and self-effacement by paying special attention to children, to the poor, and to the sick, with the freedom that engenders unselfishness in the service of the Word. Those who saw them working in this way gave them the name "reformed priests."

---

[8]Luke 17:10.

[9]Romans 8:29.

[10]John 10:10.

[11]Philippians 2:5-11.

Theirs was a completely interior reformation, even though it necessarily manifested itself externally in practices that were evidence of a renewal of their way of life; it was an interior reformation that was obedience to the Spirit and was expressed in a humble and unconditional love for the Church.

The grace of the priesthood defines the missionary service of the Society of Jesus: It is inscribed in the "hierarchical" character of the Church, which enables Jesus, as its head, to inspire, to guide each of its members and to watch over them with the attitude of the "Good Shepherd."

When the Jesuit receives priestly ordination, he finds himself invested with this responsibility in the name of the Lord. Ordination to the priesthood gives his ministry the privileged place of participation in the mystery of Jesus. It is there that he experiences his most intense joys as well as his keenest suffering.

If mission strips him of his own initiative, does not the priesthood make plain this same self-effacement? There is no other priest but Jesus; He is the Word, the Sacrament of God, the Good Shepherd who gives His life for His sheep. Nothing can be added to His priesthood. Nevertheless, there is need to translate and exercise this priesthood for those in whom He has invested His ministry: through their hearts, their actions and their words, now passes a grace for which no man is a repository, because it belongs to God alone.

The priest, therefore, experiences a radical poverty when he submits himself to the sacerdotal work of Jesus. In the "I" which he speaks, in the "I" which he baptizes, absolves, consecrates, he knows that his individual being is, so to speak, worth *nothing* since it is not the gauge of what God alone can accomplish. Faced with the Word, which he proclaims and upon which he comments, he finds himself in the role of the disciple; he is judged by the words he preaches and the actions he performs in memory of the Lord, unable to dilute the message to fit the limits of his own experience and of his life; that is, to what he knows of himself and of his weakness. Each time he attends to the needs of any person, listens to their confidences, offers them counsel, extends to them words of comfort and consolation, he discovers the mystery of a life about which only God knows the ultimate profundity and which He alone is able to guide secretly beyond all searchings, even indeed, sometimes through blind alleys and false starts.

Therefore, the priest, poor man and sinner that he is, lives the grace of his priesthood as the need to witness to Another, to act in His name, to be the instrument of His presence. If the layman, who receives the word and sacrament and who entrusts himself to Jesus the Good Shepherd, expresses loving humility in his day-to-day activities, then this same humility, this same love, this same poverty, this same faith, must all the more be the thread that runs through the life of the minister of the Lord.

Thus, in the exercise of his priesthood, the priest hears resounding over and over again the beatitude which gives him hope: "Blessed are the poor in spirit: the kingdom of Heaven is theirs." And he discovers this kingdom day after day, hidden, yet visible in the lives of men. He is enraptured by what God does in and through them, accepting with pity their requests for pardon, their desires to be reconciled with God, their brothers and sisters, and themselves. He is in this way a privileged witness to that grace which moves the hearts of men to open up, even beyond their capacities, to the gift of God.

The other beatitudes likewise express what his experiences as a priest reveal to him about the mystery of the Kingdom. "Blessed are the pure in heart: they shall see God." Here his perspective, steeped as it is in prayer and animated by contemplation, comes face-to-face with what his eye was not able to see and recognize: God Himself at work in the sufferings and torments of man, just as He is at work in his discoveries and in his capacity for joy beyond all words. Indeed, the priest must keep his heart pure so as to be in touch with this work of God. But, is it not also true that when he finds himself encountering God that, almost in spite of himself, he is assured that the needed purification will take place—a deepening and a transformation of his attitude—so that, in his dealings with men, he will not be separated from God and His work? Indeed, the whole life of a priest is beatitude, including those parts of it characterized by the most distressing heartaches and sorrows—for example, when he stretches forth his hand at a time of what seems to be irreparable loss, or when he becomes the confidant of secrets too sad for human ears to hear or for the human heart to bear—at which moments God Himself must intervene through the priest, expressing in the first person what is proper only to God, the indispensable source of peace and mercy. Whenever he may be wearied by the happenings and the encounters of the day, broken by the dramas to which he is witness, where can the priest, who knows that he is clothed with Jesus' priesthood, find a place of rest if not close beside the Lord Himself? That is, beside Him who, knowing so well our own hearts, said: "Come to me, all you who labor and are overburdened, and I will give you rest."[12]

§4. The Brothers' Vocation

Even though "in its essence" the Society of Jesus is a clerical order, not all its members are priests. We have spoken of the apostolic formation of those who are preparing for ordination; the life of the brothers, however, does not pass through exactly the same stages. But how do we understand the differences between the fathers and brothers without getting entrapped in sociological charts? These are inadequate instruments for explaining the role of brothers within the Church. Besides, they can cause terrible misunderstandings among the members of religious congregations the day they let themselves be measured by them.

As a clerical, or priestly, order, the Society lives the priesthood as service, which, not properly belonging to anyone, defines its function entirely with respect to the priesthood of Jesus. But not all Jesuit priests are engaged in the same type of work—all are not involved directly in a pastoral assignment. So, how does the priesthood of these men function in respect to Jesus' priesthood? Jesus is the only priest; His church disposes the fruits of His ministry for the whole body of believers within the Church. Within the framework of the Church there is the Society of Jesus, which participates as a body in the ministerial priesthood of the Lord according to its charisma and tradition, consistent with its role, and in conformity with its particular limitations. Whenever anyone reflects on these facts he can see there is no room for taking credit for pretended personal qualities and for harboring self-centered vain ambitions fixed on the priestly vocation.

The man who enters the Society of Jesus offering himself and all his vigor, capacity for work, fraternal availability, and energy to the common service of the Church and of the people, but who will not be ordained to the priestly state—albeit he enters completely into the

---

[12]Matthew 11:28.

service of Jesus' priesthood—this man is called a "coadjutor brother." By his person he calls to our attention that the priesthood is a mystery, not a promotion, and by his life and work he underscores our communal poverty and our communal acceptance of Jesus the priest.

It has sometimes happened that the desire to spend one's life in the service of the Church has obscured the essential nature of the priesthood, which is totally gratuitous because it is fully divine. I do not become a priest because I feel a desire for ordination nor even because I am ready to pay the price it entails. It is not because I have gone through all the preparation necessary or that I am "more worthy" than another or that I have the "right," to receive priestly ordination. The words "right," "qualified" and all similar terms do away with the most essential characteristic of the priesthood. Since it is in the order of grace, priesthood in all its gratuity and freedom cannot be completely understood by reason alone.

But how can we sincerely live this gratuitous feature of the priesthood unless we are helped by the fraternal community we form, wherein we recognize that we are gathered together by the same Lord to live a common vocation? It is here at the heart of this fraternal community that our brothers, who, although not ordained themselves are nevertheless totally consecrated to the common apostolic work of the priestly Society of Jesus and keep before us the meaning of pure gratuity.

Shall I recount here what until now I have told only a few friends? During my third year of theology, when I was getting ready for ordination, then only a few months away, I became aware of a particular "consolation," which, it now seems to me, prepared me to accept the real meaning of the priesthood. I conceived the idea of becoming a "coadjutor brother" in the Society of Jesus. It seemed to me that performing the simplest and most humble services would present me with fewer pitfalls in my desire to offer my life totally for Jesus' priestly ministry. I really do not believe that in this desire there was any fear or anxiety, however hidden, about the prospect of my upcoming ordination. Rather, there was promise of a particular joy to be able, without self-searching, without the risk of asserting myself or of appropriating to myself what belonged to Christ, to give myself completely to what Jesus the priest wanted to accomplish today in the ministry of those whom He ordains.

Ultimately, God's will did not lead me along this path. But it seems to me that because of this experience I came to understand better the true meaning of the communal service of fathers and brothers in the Society of Jesus.

The service rendered by the coadjutor brothers is also quite diversified. Although in the past their role was often seen as one which dealt with caring for the material services so essential to the life of the Society and its communities, more recently their role encompasses a more involved participation in the apostolate. Through the service that they extend to Christian communities, and by catechizing, teaching and the like, their role has taken on many forms, all excellent, for the vitality of the body and its apostolic efficacy. Who can describe all the work and sacrifices of the brothers who went to the mission countries, and who can adequately tell of their enterprising spirit and effectiveness, the value of which was augmented by the total unselfishness that motivated their undertakings? And how many churches, dispensaries, schools have been constructed as a result of their energy, sacrifice, ability; how many printing presses or workshops of different varieties have their talents enabled them to set up and manage? Who can tell of the vital role in determining the quality of community life played by so many brothers present and active in our communities, where they assume all sorts of responsible positions? For so many of them the fidelity they give to each day's work has a special quality which is as deep and refined as the spirit of contemplation itself. And, by the joy and cheerfulness of their lives, they present a privileged manifestation of Jesus' presence: "How good, how delightful it is for all to live together like brothers."[13]

Because of the changes within the Society that have prompted some values and neglected others, there has been in a number of countries today a noticeable decline in the number of brothers. No doubt the narrowness of our hearts, so lacking in fraternal kindness, has also been a cause for this reduction. This has not been a gain for the Society of Jesus, and perhaps it has especially affected its priestly character.

Fathers and brothers. If we go back to these words, how can we best seek to understand what they mean? If we consider the fraternal relationship of all the parts of the same religious family, then all the members of the Society of Jesus are brothers and they regard themselves as such. The term "Father" refers to the priestly function

---

[13]Psalm 133:1.

confided by Christ to those who are ordained. Like Jesus, the older Son, who was sent by the Father to be head of the body which He shapes according to His own fraternal image, the priest is a witness to the Fatherhood of God. He exercises a "spiritual fatherhood" for those who benefit from his ministry. The term "Father" therefore refers in reality to that Other for whom the priest is the witness and to whom everyone looks for life and assistance because all recognize in Him the source of life and the origin of grace.

§5. Diversity of the Apostolic Mission

It is difficult to put into accurate focus the exact nature of the Society of Jesus' apostolic commitment and to state precisely how it expresses the priestly ministry. The reason is that the apostolate takes on so many different appearances. In order to describe the priestly character that specifies this apostolate, I have up until now concentrated on the pastoral aspect that involves discovering God and His continuous work in the hearts of men.

In the "Formula of the Institute," a document that predates even the redaction of the *Constitutions*, Ignatius and his first companions offered the following succinct definition of the essential characteristics of the Society:

> Whoever desires to serve as a soldier of God beneath the banner of the cross in our Society, which we desire to be distinguished by the name of Jesus, and to serve the Lord alone and the Church, His spouse, under the Roman pontiff, the vicar of Christ on earth, should, after a solemn vow of perpetual chastity, poverty, and obedience, keep what follows in mind. He is a member of a Society founded chiefly for this purpose: to strive especially for the defense and propagation of the faith and for the progress of souls in Christian life and doctrine, by means of public preaching, lectures, and any other ministration whatsoever of the word of God, and further by means of the Spiritual Exercises, the education of children and unlettered persons in Christianity, and the spiritual consolation of Christ's faithful through hearing confessions and administering the other sacraments.[14]

---

[14]"Formula of the Institute," *Constitutions* [3], 66.

In this description the priesthood is given the central place it deserves. Before all else, it is described as being indispensable for Christian formation: It is the means whereby those called in faith can open up to God's life and light. In such a program of action, preaching and ministry of the Word easily find their place, as does the ministry of giving retreats and teaching children catechism.

Needless to say, by seeing the priesthood as the focal point for the service of the Word, Ignatius was in agreement, long in advance of Vatican II, with the thoughts of the Council on the role of the priest.

Priestly mediations, however, take on a variety of forms in the Jesuit apostolate. We have already stressed the importance of cultural mediations: in teaching, through the media and other forms of communication, by various research projects and the like. Beginning with the very first chapter of this book we have also stressed that St. Ignatius's *Spiritual Exercises* is the source of inspiration for giving spiritual direction to individuals and groups. Problems specific to a given culture should also be taken into account, as well as struggles that postulate the adherence of faith to the core of Christian understanding; at the end of this chapter we shall deal more explicitly with what the Thirty-second General Congregation intended as the basic blueprint for apostolic involvement for the Jesuits of today: "the service of faith and the promotion of justice," which have a direct relevance to the various aspects in the rigorous struggle for God and for man in our times.

In this section attention should be given to yet another important point, namely the choice of ministries.

"The choice of ministries"—this was the problem Ignatius himself posed, and he attempted to resolve it by setting forth some basic principles in the *Constitutions*. Indeed, it is here that we learn that the choice for taking on a ministry should not be determined merely by the nature of the apostolic work itself. Rather, this choice should be submitted to a series of criteria, that in various ways set up a hierarchy among apostolic options that should be chosen in view both of the end to be achieved—the Kingdom of God—and of the different circumstances wherein the apostolic activity is to take place.

Briefly, then, we shall go over the criteria proposed in the *Constitutions* that deal with making the choice for the place of the apostolate, the task to be accomplished, the qualities looked for in persons intended for special works, and the manner of proceeding in taking on a mission. These criteria are still as applicable today as they were when they were written, even if the projects St. Ignatius envisaged have been modified by the vagaries of history, and even if the option for a ministry, which should constantly be reevaluated by a number of these rules, is now made in pretty much a perfunctory manner. What we have here is a most striking example of discernment, to which is added a number of objective criteria and other norms designed to appeal more to subjective feelings and spelled out for us in the *Constitutions*. Moreover, it is important to remember that during the whole course of its history, the Society of Jesus has continued to question itself on the choice of its ministries.

In 1970, when Father Arrupe set out to identify those areas where the most urgent needs demanded the Society's response, he was acting in accordance with a long tradition in the Society. At that time he singled out alongside the *Spiritual Exercises*, theological reflection, social action, education, and the mass media as the most important apostolates. A short time afterwards, the Thirty-second General Congregation made reference to Father Arrupe's list but preferred to focus all the companions' apostolic efforts on one common task: the service of faith and the promotion of justice.

There are, then, few questions more current and at the same time more traditional in the day-to-day life of the Jesuit than the questions that deal with the choice of ministries. And this is normal for an apostolic order that endeavors to tie together serving God with a lively commitment to building up the Kingdom. When we evaluate the *Constitutions*' criteria for choosing ministries, we are struck by the undeniable human and Christian wisdom they contain. This is why it is worth our while to skim over a few pages of the Seventh Part of the *Constitutions* where these criteria are found.

As far as *place* is concerned, the Jesuit ought to maintain his own complete freedom and availability. The subject will always accept an appointment "joyfully" from his superior, who, because he is superior, acts in the name "of God our Lord," to send him anywhere he thinks it expedient for him to go. The superior ought to be ready to dispatch members of the Society to all places. The only rule of prudence recommended in this matter is that the superior should ponder seriously before he orders a man to go to a place where the Church has not yet been planted.[15]

---

[15]*Constitutions* [621], 273-74.

The factors for evaluating where a man should be sent, however, allow a preference of certain places over others. The proviso is that the final selection assure "the greater service of God and the more universal good."[16]

The first criterion in evaluating this decision is an objective need: this should be based on either the number of "workers" already laboring in the apostolic vineyard or on "the misery and weakness of one's fellowmen . . . and the danger of their eternal condemnation."[17]

The second criterion centers on where the greater benefits will probably be reaped from apostolic labors: these benefits are evaluated by "the disposition among the people," the insistence they have manifested by their waiting, or by the presence there of persons who "are more capable of making progress." Consequently, people who show "a greater devotion and desire" and persons whose "condition and quality" give greater promise should be given more consideration and their expectations should be acknowledged.[18]

The third criterion takes into account historical conditions: wherever Jesuits have been active and where "indebtedness" has been contracted because of the establishment of a house or a college of the Society, or "where there are members of it who study and are the recipients of charitable deeds from those people," there, in those places, "charity demands the Society to honor her obligation of gratitude and justice.[19]

The fourth criterion is more general: "The more universal the good is, the more it is divine." For this reason, "preference ought to be given to those persons and places that, through their own improvement, become a cause that can spread the good accomplished to many others who are under their influence or are under their authority.[20] During the course of the Society's history many apostolates have been initiated in the name of this principle. This led some to conclude that the Society was "elitist"; however, the choice of the "great" or the important people was never based on their pretended

---

[16]Ibid. [618], 273.

[17]Ibid. [622a], 274.

[18]Ibid. [b].

[19]Ibid. [c], 274-75.

[20]Ibid. [d], 275.

superior value; it simply meant that the Society sought to obtain through their influence the more universal and lasting good. There is no doubt that changes within society have had their effect on the wording of the question: those who now exercise the most decisive action on society and its structures are not necessarily the "elite" of earlier days. In defining the "elite," Ignatius used the language of his era, which to some extent still has a certain worth in our own times. The "elite" were, on the one hand, "important and public persons" and on the other, "persons distinguished for learning and authority."[21] And, with an eye focused on the national as well as on the international plane of development, he invited Jesuits to take into consideration the great nations and important cities and universities when they considered choosing a place for the apostolate. One cannot deny the boldness and the broad bounds of his point of view. In a somewhat modified social force there is still something there, to inspire thought and research for present-day Jesuits.

Finally the fifth and last criterion of Ignatius's proposed guide for selecting places for the apostolate contains some of the elements of the previous criteria, particularly the third: he invites Jesuits to prefer at times working in the most hostile environments, particularly in places where the Society of Jesus has a bad reputation. In this case, however, the men sent to such a place ought to be chosen with the greatest care.[22]

After the choice of places, Ignatius poses the question of *works* to be undertaken. Once again he proceeds in the same way by evoking a series of rules, all of which according to their different and complementary angles, have a role to play in making such a choice.

The first criterion here is the greater good or importance of the work under consideration: so, for example, if one cannot simultaneously undertake works for the good of souls and that of the body, through the practice of mercy and charity, then "all the other considerations being equal, the spiritual good ought to be preferred to the bodily."[23]

---

[21]Ibid. [e].
[22]Ibid. [f].
[23]Ibid. [623a, 623b], 275-76.

The second criterion is that of greater urgency.[24]

The third, that of necessity. The gauge here is the degree of neglect given to certain works that no one else wants and no one is looking for ways to provide.[25]

According to the terms of the fourth criterion, "among the pious works of equal importance, urgency, and need," those that are safer for the one who cares for them" should be preferred to those that pose a risk, and works that "are easier and more quickly dispatched" should be preferable to others "more difficult and finished only in a longer time."[26]

In the perspective of the fifth criterion, when all the preceding criteria are of equal worth, normally one should give priority to works that affect a larger number of persons, such as preaching and teaching, as opposed to works that are limited to a smaller number of persons, such as hearing confessions or giving the Exercises.[27]

The sixth criterion gives special value to "spiritual works that continue longer and are of more lasting value, such as certain pious foundations for the aid of our fellowmen," as opposed to works less durable and "that give help on a few occasions and only for a short time.[28]

The choice of *persons* who are to be sent is the next item that occupies Ignatius's attention. He proposes a few new general principles. First of all, because one must avoid error in all cases, men should be chosen according to their suitability and promise. When a mission demands greater physical industry, one should select men who are stronger and healthier.[29] Where there is a spiritual risk involved, one should appeal to men who are "more approved in virtue and more reliable."[30] If it is a question of making contact with individuals who are blessed with discretion and are responsible for "spiritual or temporal government," the superior should select "the most suitable [men] who excel in discretion and grace of conversa-

---

[24]Ibid. [c], 276.

[25]Ibid. [d].

[26]Ibid. [e].

[27]Ibid. [f].

[28]Ibid. [g].

[29]Ibid. [624a, 624b], 276-77.

[30]Ibid. [c], 277.

tion and . . . have a pleasing appearance that increases their prestige."[31] "[W]ith cultivated persons of talent and learning," one normally should dispatch men who have "a special gift of skill and learning."[32] The making up of teams should receive the highest consideration by trying to select men for the same mission who have complementary talents.[33]

As far as the purpose of sending men is concerned, there should be no other purpose than "the greater edification of the neighbor and the service of God our Lord."[34]

Even from this very dry recital of criteria for taking on apostolic works one can see that if the Society of Jesus does not define itself by a specified type of work, by serving this or that country on this or that continent, or this or that class of people, the reason is that it is dedicated totally to the service of Jesus' priesthood according to the universal dimension with which it invests its ministry. This principle is the source of the extraordinary diversity of apostolic commitments that Jesuits take on; it is the origin of that impressive missionary spirit which has animated the Society of Jesus from its very beginnings and throughout the course of its history. The "fourth vow" of obedience to the Roman pontiff regarding "the missions" throws light on the composite parts of this apostolic universalism.

§6. The "Fourth Vow": Obedience to the Pope

Like all religious, Jesuits take a vow of poverty, chastity, and obedience. In doing so they give witness to the ultimate dimensions of man in his relation to the world, to his fellow man, and to God. Moreover, as in the case of a number of other religious congregations, the Society of Jesus has a fourth vow, one that says something more specific about the meaning of the Jesuit vocation. In order to understand the significance and implications of this vow, it is again necessary to go back to the experience of Ignatius and his first companions. On August 15, 1534, while still in Paris, they went to Montmartre and

---

[31]Ibid. [d].

[32]Ibid. [e].

[33]Ibid. [f].

[34]Ibid. [625], 278.

there, in addition to taking a vow of poverty, and perhaps also of chastity, they made the vow to go to Jerusalem, where they would spend themselves in the service of souls. When they made this promise, they had the foresight to place on it this condition: in case they were prevented from going to Jerusalem, they vowed to present themselves to the "vicar of Christ" in Rome, and there place themselves at his service to do with them whatever he decided proper for the glory of God and the good of souls.

Then, three years later, in 1537, after receiving earlier that same year Pope Paul III's permission to be ordained by any bishop, even though they were without either "benefice" or diocese, they were ordained in Venice "in title of their voluntary poverty and sufficient learning." Here they tarried, looking for an opportunity to leave for the Holy Land. Their waiting, however, was in vain and so they had to fall back on the second part of their missionary vow: they had to place themselves at the service of the Holy Father. The text in the *Constitutions* plainly and distinctly retains the memory of these events. It recalls how the first companions' recourse to the pope was the expression of their desire to rely on him who, from a universal point of view, was best able to give direction to their priestly mission.

> For those who first united to form the Society were from different provinces and realms and did not know into which regions they were to go whether among the faithful or unbelievers; and therefore, to avoid erring in the path of the Lord, they made that promise or vow in order that His Holiness might distribute them for the greater glory of God.[35]

And again, by insisting more precisely on the missionary mobility of their vow, which the first companions wanted to be the driving power of their lives, the *Constitutions* stress the fact that they made this vow:

> in conformity with their intention to travel throughout the world and, when they could not find the desired spiritual fruit in one region, to pass on to another and another ever intent on seeking the greater glory of God our Lord and the greater aid of souls.[36]

---

[35]*Constitutions* [605], 268.
[36]Ibid.

Such was the experience out of which came the Jesuits' fourth vow, a vow which bears a "special obedience to the sovereign pontiff in regard to the missions."[37] It is important here to emphasize this fact: the experience which gave birth to the fourth vow is anterior to the setting up of the Society of Jesus as a religious order. This fact enables us to understand the sense in which Ignatius and his first companions understood this fourth vow as the "principle and foundation" of their Society. When the *Constitutions* deal with the subject of the Society's mission, they do not explicitly state that the Sovereign Pontiff is its primary source of reference, even though frequently—and indeed almost always—superiors in the Society in one way or another have to determine in his name the work or ministry their brothers are to undertake.

We have already discussed how, even though not all Jesuits are ordained priests, nevertheless all participate in the sacerdotal mission of the body of the Society. In the same fashion, not all Jesuits take the fourth vow but all are pledged in solidarity and fraternity to a company of men which, in the last analysis receives its mission and the specifics of that mission from the pope, who is unique witness to the universal body of believers rooted in the priesthood of Christ Jesus.

Some writers have claimed that the origin of the fourth vow is the fact that Jesuits wanted to constitute a special body of troops at the service of the pope. Not so at all. The pope is not a temporal sovereign like other rulers; nor was he so in the sixteenth century. He does not need a militia of troops, as that term is understood. Nor does he have his own special, private agenda to pursue. As for Ignatius, he always distinguished with the greatest precision between a spiritual and material good, and he certainly had no intention of ever introducing a partisan spirit into the Church. If the fourth vow ties individual Jesuits and the whole Society of Jesus to the pope, it does so precisely to strip from individual Jesuits and the Society all forms of particularism by inscribing their total mission within the universal sacerdotal mission of the Church.

Today the fourth vow, like the priesthood, is calculated to create a kind of scandal. But the fact is that if we want to come out clearly in favor of the way the Church understands the priesthood, we must

---

[37]Ibid. [527], 238.

transcend a certain skepticism and fuzzy thinking peculiar to our times. Very likely too, we have to overcome a number of temptations to espouse particularism and subjectivism if we honestly want to choose to have a special bond with the bishop of Rome and, through him, with the whole hierarchical Church.

Moreover, it should be borne in mind that there is nothing more opposed to the Ignatian spirit than the all too frequent opposition we see today between the Church as community and the Church as institution. Most assuredly during Ignatius's time it was no easier than it is today for people to see in the institutional Church the transparency of the mystery of grace which she is supposed to make available to man. But God's mystery is not detected by human eyes; the Father's continuous love transcends what can be perceived within the scope of the human spectrum. God, who willed to reveal Himself to us in his Son Jesus, has not ceased coming into our lives today through the sacraments. His glory manifests its presence in the sacraments of the Church. Today, just as it was in the past, it is in the sacraments and in the Word, of which the Church is the custodian and the herald, where the vision of faith converges with the definitive meaning of the institutional Church.

Ignatius's vision of the Church, which one can find reflected in the *Exercises* as well as in the *Constitutions of the Society of Jesus,* is that she is the spouse of Christ and the mother of Christians. It is in this hierarchical Church, or in the terms of Ignatius, in "our Holy Mother, the hierarchical Church,"[38] that the Jesuit discovers his identity as Jesuit, and it is here where he desires to vow himself totally—which he does, when he promises the pope a special obedience in respect to the missions.

The "Formula of the Institute," wherein are contained the essential elements of the Society which were approved by the Church, gives the reasons for making this vow of obedience: the Society sees in such a vow the expression of a fuller fidelity to the Apostolic See, the manifestation of greater renunciation, and the surer guarantee of being led by the Spirit. What this means for the Society of Jesus, which receives as a result of this vow its particular place in the Lord's Church, is a willingness to sacrifice totally its own agenda in order to

---

[38]*The Spiritual Exercises* [353], 157. This is a reference to the first "rule to be observed to foster the true attitude of mind we ought to have in the church militant."

be sent by the Spirit to whatever place it pleases the successor of Peter to send its members. Such a putting off of self in total abandonment and in faith is necessarily the source of both suffering and joy; in the practical order this renunciation translates itself in the manner in which Jesuits as a group place themselves in the paschal mystery of Jesus; that is, by living both the essence of their religious commitment and offering up the totality of their persons to the Lord's priesthood, a priesthood which is specified hierarchically in His Church.

From the very beginning Ignatius saw Jerusalem as the privileged place of mission because it was in Jerusalem that the Word of God was preached before being carried off to the ends of the earth. When he placed himself at the service of the Roman pontiff, he continued to put into operation the same logic, the same faith in the Word Incarnate. The "Vicar of Christ" would be henceforth his point of reference for a mission that had to be lived universally according to the very injunction of Jesus to go out to the whole world, proclaiming the Good News to all nations. The diversity of ministries in the Society has no other justification than this still point of the turning world, this center, where its reason for being has its origin. Moreover, this same commitment to the priestly mission of the universal Church, symbolized in the Roman pontiff, is the compelling force for the missionary mobility of the Jesuits. This attachment to the universal Church does not in any way draw Jesuits away from serving the particular church where they work. On the contrary, by drawing power from the personal commitment they bear to the universal Church, Jesuits desire only to dedicate themselves with all of their affections to the local church where obedience has sent them, desiring nothing more than to be men who work in union with the whole Church by disposing each one of the faithful to receive the gift of the Word and the sacraments wherein the loving humility and the efficacious gift of the Lord shines in glory for all His people.

§7. The Jesuits' Missionary Freedom

We have spoken of freedom in regard to the Jesuit's mission. In the last analysis this is a freedom which goes hand-in-hand with the total acceptance of obedience. When is it possible for me to feel more free than when I know I am where God wants me to be, doing His work in the place He has designated for me? Christian obedience is an experience of freedom; and so it is with religious obedience.

When Ignatius, together with his companions, first founded an order that was basically missionary, he came to realize the importance of providing it with certain safeguards that would guarantee freedom for its apostolic works. In working out the overall plan to preserve this freedom, he was prompted more by the example set by Jesus and His apostles during the course of the public life of our Lord than he was by any common sense organizational pattern. He believed there was no clearer model for understanding the demands of a life totally dedicated to mission work than the example of Jesus and His apostles.

However, from the very beginning, the first Jesuits had agreed that there were some specific ministries in which they would not become involved. They would not take charge of women religious; they would accept ecclesiastical offices and titles only at the expressed command of the pope, and they would exempt themselves from reciting the Divine Office in choir, which at that time was seen to be an essential element of the religious life. They justified making these decisions on the basis of their determination to be free to give themselves unreservedly to their apostolic mission. They bore no contempt for, and they had no negative judgments about, these apostolates they decided to exclude. They simply perceived that a different type of vocation, the one they had chosen, called for a different set of criteria, and that was the set they adopted.

With the history of the Society behind us, we are in a better position today to appreciate reasons prompting the first fathers to decide what legitimate forms of the apostolate threatened their missionary freedom. It would indeed be unfair to reproach Jesuits for having no interest in the life of women religious. Over the course of the years many congregations of religious women have come into existence through the inspiration of the Society's spirituality and constitutions, and these groups have sought aid and assistance from Jesuits. Ignatius's directive regarding the charge of religious women was to avoid having Jesuits become involved in a long-term commitment. It was not meant to prohibit the Society from extending fraternal and friendly support. It is a matter of record that throughout the years the Society's assistance has promoted independence and self-governance among religious women's congregations that the Lord has caused to spring up in His Church for His glory. From the very beginning the priestly grace of the Society has taught how

Jesuits should take on pastoral responsibility for individuals and communities. It consistently employs this same criterion of freedom along with a concern to awaken in every individual an authentically honest response to freedom.

Secondly, it is contrary to Ignatius's spirit for a Jesuit to nourish the slightest ambition for any ecclesiastical dignity, and most particularly for the office of bishop. The reason for this is that the Jesuit should maintain a special type of humility in his service to the Church, and he should try to avoid a permanent assignment to serve the Church in a particular area because through its availability and mobility the Society of Jesus is committed to serving whatever the universal Church wants in many different ways.

Finally, there was the decision that Jesuits were not to recite the Divine Office together in choir. The pilgrim of Manresa, who had learned to accommodate his prayer to suit the recitation of the Divine Office, could not have come hastily to this decision. Moreover, isn't it true that the hours Ignatius recommended in the *Spiritual Exercises* for the retreatant's meditations correspond to those more extended periods of time when the monks were not in choir singing the office? The fact is that if the apostolate forces a Jesuit to take on a schedule which is frequently quite irregular, he cannot arrange his daily life to synchronize with the customary rhythm of reciting Divine Office in choir. How would a contemplative soul not be able to savor the beneficent effects which refresh the spirit and even the body itself during the recitation of the Divine Office? Do not the church bell that punctually calls me to prayer and the recitation of the Office help me to perceive how much the Word of God, the praise, and the adoration centered in choir are able to open up my life to a Presence which transcends that life and at the same time gives it a structure? How can I not feel a kind of outpouring of sentiments and a purification of the carnal man penetrating me whenever I conform to that discipline of a prayer continuously renewed, a prayer which gives to my day's work and activity strong undergirdings and the quickening of my spirit in God himself? There is no doubt about it, one has to have relished and appreciated the support of the liturgy of the hours sung in choir to understand what giving up this place of praise and adoration really means in the life of a Jesuit. But in order that this renunciation may not translate itself into a loss of interior devotion and an illusory freedom, a freedom merely from some extrinsic coercion, it is also necessary that the needs of the apostolate and the demands of the mission manifest in a different mode the same inflooding of the Other to whom the Jesuit has unreservedly vowed his life and in whom he wishes to lose himself. The glory of God has to surge up in his life, not only as a focal point of that light which makes everything clear, but more as a fire to which he surrenders himself, in the complete loss of self, so that he is always waiting on God and the needs of the Kingdom to communicate to him the Life and the Word. This is true liberty, but it is always a heavy, laborious liberty: it drains the heart and its very interests—including the attachment to those interests. It is a liberty that can keep the heart free for the gentle and peace-bringing experience of God.

We have referred to the demands of the mission. Ever since the earliest days, this was an exigency profoundly felt and was the reason that so many men left for far-off lands. It was from Rome, where he kept up his interest in all of Europe, as well as in Asia, Africa, and America, that Ignatius strove to remain in communion with the length and breadth of the whole worldwide mission. And it is striking today to see with what a sense of freedom the first Companions launched out on the highways of the world to announce the Gospel of Christ. The Church, which they were pledged to serve, was the Church spread far and wide, the Church which was to be planted on every continent and which ever found itself involved in new fields of apostolic endeavor. The provinces, which today testify to the presence of the Society of Jesus in almost every country of the world, trace their beginnings to the eagerness with which the Companions set forth to traverse the whole world, bearing in their hearts the hope of the Kingdom and the urgency to announce Christ to all their brothers and sisters.

This same universality of mission calls for a dialogue today, for a mutual exchange of ideas and opinions between the various provinces of the Society. The Society's general superior is in the habit of calling different superiors or teams of men who head different apostolic works to Rome, and he himself travels about to assist at province assemblies or at important meetings organized at the regional level. Unity is thereby constantly rediscovered in diversity, a unity which is really no different from the unity of the Church itself and from that missionary service to which the Companions have vowed themselves.

Because the notion of missionary universality encourages the rotation of men, and the diffusion of information and ideas throughout the Society, it is at variance with the policy of restricting Jesuits to working solely in their own countries or provinces. Missionary universality keeps alive that liberty which the Society of Jesus must have in order to be faithful to its tradition and history.

§8. Missionary Obedience

The role of obedience is crucial in a missionary corps as diverse as the Society of Jesus in order to guarantee unity of direction and mutual cooperation in the realization of its mission. In 1539 when Ignatius and his companions deliberated together on the advisability of adding the vow of obedience to those of poverty and chastity, which they had already taken in Venice at the time of their priestly ordination, they were, in effect, discussing whether or not they should form a new religious order. We have indicated that before this date they had already promised that they would place themselves at the disposal of the pope in regard to the missions, a promise which later would become the fourth vow in the Society of Jesus. Then, after prayer and reflection, they decided that they would stay together as a group united through their apostolic labors; that they would form a corps which gradually, under God's Providence, came into being. Finally they committed themselves to "give obedience to one among them." At a later date, Ignatius would be elected the first superior general of the Society of Jesus.

This is the same Ignatius who on several occasions would lay stress on this vow of obedience and on the unique position he held as general of the new religious order. His function in the order became pivotal for the existence and vitality of an apostolic group whose mission (the act of being sent) was the determining element.

We have already seen that the Jesuit lives out his freedom joyfully and serenely in his self-surrender to the will of him who sends him on mission, a will not regarded in its human dimensions but as a mediation of the very will of God Himself. So that I can be sure of stretching out over the whole course of my life this act of sending, which finds its origin in the salvific mission of the Word and the Spirit, I surrender myself with gratitude to the word which determines my field of action, my assignment, my responsibility in "the vineyard of the Lord." For me this word is the Word of God. By so surrendering himself to obedience the Jesuit is singularly "lucky."[39] Through obedience he is assured of being in conformity with the love which is at the source of his vocation. Through obedience he has the assurance he is committed to a project which goes beyond him, but one in which he has his place and for which, in a sense, God depends on him; that is, God relies on his collaboration and commitment. Through obedience then, he weds himself, joyfully, to the sometimes crucifying word from his superior, the word that guarantees he will achieve the disposition to conform the most profound dynamic element of his person and liberty to God's will.

Such an obedience at the service of the mission requires both dialogue and a more than ordinary mutual trust between the one who sends and the one who is sent. The Society of Jesus has always defended the union of these two elements so proper to Ignatian obedience in the "account of conscience." He who in God's name sends me on mission, thereby subjecting me to his command to take on an assignment, has to know very well who I am and where grace is leading me. He should be aware of my weaknesses and temptations as well as my hopes and expectations. Without this knowledge, how could he honestly say to me: Do this, it is the Lord Himself who entrusts it to you? How could he tell me with assurance what the concrete form my missionary vocation is taking unless the two of us together had not first tried to recognize it through the way it manifested itself within me, unless my superior was aware of how I have been getting along in my present assignment and how I regard this present apostolate to which I have been sent?

It is for this reason that before ever being an exercise in asceticism, obedience for the Jesuit is a fraternal dialogue with a view to achieving honest discernment and attaining God's will in an assignment to a mission. The primary intention of the superior is not to organize his apostolic forces simply in view of a specific project. And his assignment of personnel is based upon something completely different from a simple need for manpower distribution or from measuring out resources so that some determined undertaking might take form. Undoubtedly the "apostolic work" in which I participate can raise me above myself and can justify the superior's enlisting me

---

[39]Dominque Bertrand, *Un corps pour l'ésprit.* Colléction Christus (Paris: Desclée De Brouwer, 1974), 150 et seq.

and my abilities for a work which does not correspond to what I would spontaneously choose for an assignment. However, the giving up of my own preference, a relinquishment which can sometimes be painful, is not a natural reaction. All the same, it is not contrary to a prior choice which I have already made. This prior choice is a more fundamental act of my will and it includes my capacity for making commitments and sacrifices. It makes possible the dialogue in which I obediently reveal myself, with all of my interior feelings and inclinations, to my superior so that God may dispose of me according to my nature and abilities.

When one calls attention to the central role obedience enjoys in the Society of Jesus, he sometimes risks confining it to an external description, likening it to the nature of military or administrative obedience. The revelation of "the account of conscience" puts such a conception in stark contrast with what is the most personal experience possible. If I have been able to open myself honestly to the one who orders my life, the one who sends me in God's name to my particular apostolate, then I know that he is aware of me as I am, with all of my strengths and weaknesses, my virtues and shortcomings, and that he has taken into account the spiritual struggle of the assignment I might be given as well as the voice of the Spirit within me. This mission is given to me by God through the mediation of the superior and it becomes mine. I know that it will open up my life to the way of the Lord, that it will place me in his service, and I accept it generously without holding anything back. Far from being bullied by the superior's order, the spirited enthusiasm for my enterprise, the unqualified resolution of my energies are somehow liberated and confirmed. Obedience sends me, all of me; the mission demands every part of me. And once my superior gives me that mission, there is no conceivable doubt, no holding back, no possible deception, no other expectation or hope to foster.

§9. The Service of Faith and the Promotion of Justice

On May 7, 1965, during the course of the Thirty-first General Congregation, which elected Father Pedro Arrupe general superior of the order, Pope Paul VI addressed an allocution to the assembled fathers, in which he asked that the Society of Jesus assume responsibility for the fight against atheism.[40] The Sovereign Pontiff was profoundly affected by the contemporary drama of "atheistic humanism," and he asked the Jesuits to meet this challenge in their work of evangelization and Christian education. However, responding to such an appeal is not an easy matter because a theoretical knowledge of atheism is not enough, much less is there sufficient will to obey this mission the Pope confided to the Society. The apostle who takes on such a mission must understand totally—that is, with all his mind, all his will, all his heart—the present condition of today's world with its gradual drifting away from religious faith and its tendency to obfuscate values, whereby it threatens what is most essential for man's salvation. While clearly seeing all of this, he must at the same time perceive with the same deep-felt awareness, even to the point of letting the enormity of it cause him actual pain, the thirst the crucified Lord expressed to communicate His life, to go in search of all those given to Him, to open them in the Spirit to the presence and gift of the Father, and to snatch them from the darkness of a world shut up in its own false self-complacency.

Every apostle lives out this drama in his life today—some more than others because of the particular country in which they live. He participates in it whenever he listens to people who share their confidences with him, whenever he observes and understands how men, whom Christ infinitely loves and has saved, live their lives. At times, he feels within himself the full weight that the combat for God has imposed on our contemporaries. His temptation might be to take refuge in a work more immediately at hand, in his everyday job, and in this way hope to acquire a good conscience from the regular performance of a set routine. Isn't there a certain risk involved in letting oneself be inundated by the devastating waves of disbelief? There are some who manage to drown in them, others who lose their landmarks and end up hurt or skeptical. Granted, it is better not to forejudge one's strength but to be faithful to the commitment one has undertaken, to deal with those who dwell within the limitations of one's own abilities, and to work with people who are less liable to dismay one or make one's head swim with their arguments.

---

[40]Address of His Holiness Pope Paul VI to the Members of the 31st General Congregation, May 7, 1965. *Documents of the 31st and 32d General Congregations of the Society of Jesus*, 311-16.

Nevertheless, the invitation comes back again and again, insistent, imperious, as a call which wells up from the very heart of Christ Himself, a call which Pope Paul VI, the one we recognized as Christ's "vicar on earth" took up by entrusting to us this mission in His name.

In virtue of the Pope's allocution, the Society of Jesus and its provinces have made some important policy changes, even though there has been some hesitation that momentarily has slowed up this drive. There has been a more conscious awareness of anything in our time that threatens the integrity of the faith and questions its contents, both within and outside the Church, or that denies the true nature of God and His Christ, or the nature of man, the object of His kindness.

The Thirty-second General Congregation came together at the behest of Paul VI. In its earnest endeavor to accept the mission that he had entrusted to the Society ten years earlier (to offer resistance to the many forms of contemporary atheism), the Congregation determined to mobilize more of the Society's energies to show with more force how seriously it took Paul VI's commission "as a modern expression of your vow of obedience to the Pope."[41]

In response to the Pope's challenge, the Congregation focussed the basic orientation of the Society's total apostolate on "the service of the faith." At the same time, it added to this task of "service of the faith," the notion of "the promotion of justice" as a priority of capital importance for its mission in the contemporary world.[42]

The clear decision for the Society's mission today was spelled out by the Congregation in its fourth decree, "Our Mission Today: The Service of Faith and the Promotion of Justice." What precisely is the meaning of this decree which purports to give in most concrete terms the missionary guidelines of the Society of Jesus in our time? It is an extended reflection from the *Spiritual Exercises* on what Ignatius asks the retreatant to consider in the contemplation on the Incarnation of the Son of God. From the very beginning of God's salutary

---

[41]Address of His Holiness Pope Paul VI to the Members of the 32d General Congregation, December 3, 1974, Ibid., 519-36.

[42]In the treatment of this subject, the General Congregation explicitly referred to declarations of "the past two synods of bishops." Ibid., 422. "Justice in the World," text of the 1971 Synod of Bishops in *The Pope Speaks*, 16 (1972) 377-81 and "Evangelization in the Modern World," The Apostolic Exhortation of Pope Paul based on the vast collection of speeches and declarations made by more than two hundred bishops who participated in the 1974 Synod of Bishops. *The Pope Speaks*, 21 (1976), 4-51.

decision, He looked down upon man with love and hope, upon the whole expanse of all the earth, filled with human beings in need of salvation. Now if we attempt to adapt God's vision to the men of our day, what unfolds before our eyes is the tragic condition of humanity of which we are a part. Added to, and intertwined with, the spiritual drama of man's refusal to acknowledge God's existence, or of his lack of desire to know Him, is the human drama of the hatred and destruction of our fellow human beings. Today there is much evil that undermines human society and relations between men. Many people are victims of hate or injustice and end up torn apart, lost, and abandoned to a sterile, death-bearing fate. So often man is a wolf toward man. His blind appetite for sensual enjoyment and his equally blind desire for power, which destroy the respect every man ought to have for his brother, keep him awake on his bed at night plotting ways to abuse with disdain the image of God each person bears within the inmost depths of his being. How are we able today to collaborate in the redemptive work of Christ for each one of His brothers if we have not nourished in our heart of hearts a tender and grieving love for the least of the Lord's little ones who have been barred from partaking in the goods of this world and deprived of their rights as human beings?

Of course, it is not easy to keep alive in one's heart these demands of charity, to hear continuously from every quarter and to pay genuine attention to "the cry of the poor" while one is an active participant in the social and political life of the privileged citizens of the land. For this reason, during the past few years many Jesuits have been sent to live as witnesses of the faith and proclaimers of the Gospel of salvation in the midst of the poor, in a human solidarity designed to awaken a greater sense of responsibility in the combat for a greater world.

When one begins to dedicate himself to this combat, it is perhaps likewise difficult to keep his heart open solely to those techniques and laws that are found in Jesus' Gospel. It is in this situation also that the Jesuit must resolve to purify his heart to open himself to the truth of the Kingdom which is to come, to mercy and peace in the very midst of suffering.

Yes, the service of faith and the promotion of justice. But when Jesuits state the direction of their mission today, they want to remain faithful to Ignatian inspiration, particularly as it is expressed in the "Formula of the Institute." The Society of Jesus, as a clerical order committed to proclaiming the Gospel and educating others in the way of faith and Christian living, is intent on fulfilling its mission by being present to man as he is today with all his pain and sufferings. The "Formula of the Institute" offers a guideline here because to such recommended apostolic priestly ministries as preaching and dispensing the sacraments, it adds the ministry of service and charity. From the very earliest days, were not Ignatius and his companions eager to serve the sick and prisoners, to visit hospitals and prisons? Man, sick and bereft of his freedom, is in the midst of our cities and societies so that now we can come to him to be near him. In coming to know him better and love him more, we want to learn from him and to discover with him the ways we should travel together in order to transform the world so it can correspond better with man's nature and Jesus' Gospel. The Jesuit's desire is not to become a substitute for political officials. Rather, what he wants is to be a witness, a prophet in the social environment of our times by re-echoing the Word which judges all of us, raises us up, and saves us; by accepting whatever the price he may have to pay to be a witness to this Word of truth and to the demands it imposes on everyone, and also by attempting, if he has acquired any expertise in such matters, to throw light on the economic, social, or political problems of our times. At all times what the Jesuit does is done to serve man more fully and to give God greater glory.

Our discussion of the steps that led to the decisions made in the Thirty-second General Congregation regarding the combat against atheism and our commitment to faith and justice have left us with insufficient space to give a detailed description of the generosity of the many good men who have joyfully volunteered to pledge themselves, even at times to the point of putting their own lives on the block, to serve Christ because their faith in God has exacted from them a particular love for man as well as a desire to serve Christ in His suffering members and in the poorest of the poor. And, if at times we have let ourselves be overcome by the uncertainty of the struggle or if our discernment has lacked courage and daring, may the Lord come to our assistance, and may He give our mission and our companions the assurance of His presence and the presence of His Spirit in this world of ours, which we are able to love with all our hearts because, in the truest sense of the word, it is first and foremost His world.

IV

The Apostolic Corps of the Society of Jesus

§1. A Missionary Community

When the Companion of Jesus enters religious life, he is immediately introduced to community life. He does not vow himself to the Lord alone, nor does he answer His invitation to take on the mission alone, in isolation from his brothers. He attaches himself to a missionary group, a community, a corps. This fact, which is intrinsic to the concept of Jesuit obedience, gives the rationale for the so-called "deliberation of the first fathers." Rather than remaining isolated individuals in their priestly mission to the universal Church, the first companions—Ignatius and his friends—chose to live together in total dependence on one another, intent on working together for a common cause even when eventually the demands of ministry would separate and scatter them.

This historic decision, so important in the collective memory of the Society, sheds light on why today the young Companion of Jesus learns to become a part of a community; to place his work, studies, and apostolic commitment within the framework of the whole corps, the collective body which transcends himself and all his efforts. Once he makes the choice to live this community life, his obedience and his association with his brothers ensure his attachment to all the members of the corps and at the same time guarantee his own personal development. As we have already seen, the Society of Jesus is a missionary community. This means that the Society does not depend upon the stability of a group established in a particular place, from which prayer and evangelical hospitality radiate. The Society of Jesus is not a monastic community of brothers that God gathers together in a permanent way under an abbot, a father, or an elder who symbolizes the mutual commitment of religious to a particular monastery that death alone can sever.

Or let us express the Jesuit's vocation in another way. If our life includes an irretrievably mutual commitment similar to that found in a monastery, it does so only in respect to the whole body of the Society, which does not own its existence to being gathered together in a particular place. The Thirty-second General Congregation reminded us that the Jesuit community "is the entire body of the Society itself, no matter how widely dispersed over the face of the earth. The particular local community to which [the Jesuit] may belong at any given moment is, for him, simply a concrete—if here and now, a privileged—expression of this worldwide brotherhood."[1] If this "community in dispersion" finds its "concrete expression" in a particular mission, it will also derive its coherence from the sincere commitment each member makes to the task entrusted to him.

For a man to live together with others in community, he must first cultivate within himself a capacity for brotherly attachment to others, the ability to listen to them and to show them respect, and to deal with them sincerely and honestly. He must foster the capacity for friendship and care for others, for understanding, goodwill, and forgiveness. He must be able to join in common prayer with his brothers and converse with them about life in the community and about the community's apostolate. He does this when he reflects, considers, and discerns with them what is of benefit to each one in the community. In order for a man to do all of this, he must be able to silence thoughts of egoism and selfish independence as well as the temptation to isolate himself from others; he must be able to transcend prejudices that smack of factions or closed-mindedness. All of these essential conditions for living in fraternity, however, are not enough for the type of apostolic community that the Society of Jesus envisions.

Once I have settled in and have become completely attached to my brothers, I ought to be ready at any time to pull up stakes and leave them, if this is what I am asked to do. I must then go off to join another community of different Jesuits. There I should begin anew with the same enthusiasm and the same determination to build community on foundations and in an environment perhaps totally

---

[1] *Documents of the 31st and 32d General Congregations* [26], 404.

different from the community I have left. Such is the price I pay for apostolic mobility, for the freedom of being committed to the missionary life. Now, how do I go about reconciling these two essential requisites of Jesuit life: readiness to move from one place to another and fulfillment in companionship with my brothers? These two requisites define the fundamental characteristic of what is true about living as a Companion of Jesus.

During my life as a Jesuit, I can be sent on mission to places that differ considerably one from another. At one time I can be assigned to a community of four or five men, then sent to one of more than a hundred. In my different assignments I can meet many brothers with whom I can work for the evangelization of the world. In every place I should be able to feel "at home" with the same kind of freedom. The place I call "my community" is not a world unto itself nor is it a house for a tightly knit clique. Rather, it is primarily a community open to all those other places throughout the world that reflect my own obedience to be sent to a designated mission.[2] Each community is a place from which I should be able to have a worldwide view.

A man who lives in such a community experiences both the warmth of friendship, which can be developed with confidence because it is the product of a shared vocation, and the harsh austerity of loneliness intrinsic to accepting the state of being uprooted. These are the very sentiments that remind the apostle over and over again who he is and who it is that he has chosen to serve. They purify his intentions; they assure his integrity, and they demand that he be ever friendly and always at the service of the brothers among whom he lives.

It well may be that we have become too much accustomed to seeing our dealings with others in community from a unidimensional point of view, one that puts great emphasis on "my rights" that have to be defended and guaranteed. Such an attitude has been the undoing of more than one Jesuit, and it is why some have been plunged into deepest desolation. A man may ask: Does the community where I live give me what I expect, what I have the right to demand from it? However, if we pose the question this way we forget that the brotherhood we share is rooted in the gratuity of love and that everything that one receives in community is a gift which is never merited. It is

---

[2]Cf. *Constitutions* [304, 588], 169-70, 262-63.

an expression, a revelation of God's own kindness. Thinking in this selfish way also indicates I have lost sight of the fact that my love is a fire which consumes me and which invites me to forget myself in giving without counting the cost, in offering myself to each one without ever expecting anything in return. To live an authentic community life, in the place where the Lord has sent me, means that I make the law of charity my own. That law is the sum and substance of the Gospel. It requires that I lose my life for all my brothers and sisters, beginning with those who are closest to me, those with whom I share the same roof and table. If I am not imbued with this attitude, how will I ever be able to announce the infinite love of God without trembling? Furthermore, every time during the day my brothers accept me and welcome me as they would the Lord Himself, I am invited to be overwhelmed by joy and feelings of gratitude for all that has been given to the poor man I am with such simplicity and generosity. Such a habit of mind calls for discretion, forgetfulness of self, respect for others, and a willingness to forgive others. And what I receive in turn are the consolation and joy of the "poor in spirit" for all that is given them—gifts in which they can recognize love.

All the different kinds of Jesuit community life should express themselves in a panoply of activities, actions, and rites, the symbolic value and regular repetition of which are assurances to the individual Jesuit of his belonging to the group and of being open to the world at large, that world which gives meaning to his very vocation and to his mission as a Jesuit. In this matter the long-accepted policy in the Society of Jesus has been to allow considerable latitude for adapting a particular panoply of community functions. We have already seen that Jesuits do not chant the Divine Office in choir because there should be no compromise made when it comes to apostolic freedom. This same freedom is always meant to be relative to circumstances, such as the place where the community is situated, the demands of the times, and the type of apostolic work in which the community is involved. These are the factors that will inspire the adaptation of distinct ways and different schedules of activities designed to sustain community life. But in one way or another, prayer will always find its place among the scheduled events because prayer guarantees the Jesuit's perfect forgetfulness of himself and of his particular projects. This is true especially of the Mass, the great prayer of Jesus, His Eucharist, the source of our unity and communion. Moreover, every type of community discussion, whether in a formal or relaxed setting, will always seek to discover the ways that promise to nourish the life of each member of the community as well as to guarantee that the community will really be what it is meant to be. Provided that the community is faithful to what it should be, these discussions will lead to a discernment of what the Lord wants. But even in those times when the community is not consciously aware of how to form itself, it is the ordinariness of what people say and do on a daily basis that puts together most effectively the bonds that unite the companions in a brotherhood. Day after day, each of us in the community can thank the Lord humbly and faithfully for what He has given us through so many of our brothers. At those times when God wills to come to me in my weakness, how much support, advice, and encouragement have I not been given by the brothers whom He has placed along my route? Without these men it would be impossible for me to carry on the mission He has given me in the service of His Church.

We have described the essential points in Jesuit community life and what it takes to live that life. But it is also important to keep in mind that community life lived on the local level in the Society of Jesus is not defined or limited by the needs and aspirations of the community itself. The interior spiritual life of the particular community, as well as the mutual interest, concern, and care that life reflects, is extended first to all the communities within a given province or region and then to the whole body of the Society itself.

It is a marvel of God's grace that men who do not know one another and who frequently live great distances from one another, are able to forge themselves into a true community, sharing the same spirit, members all of the same corps. This fact becomes evident when a man travels to different houses, or attends intercontinental meetings; or when by chance one Jesuit meets another. Despite all of the differences that separate us—age, national origins, formation, apostolates—the unity proper to our "religious family" is something that is deeply rooted in our spirit. This is so because of the working of the Holy Spirit. This unity enables the Jesuit to travel throughout the world and yet always feel in a sense at home among other Jesuits. One might say that this is the compensation for the need to be mobile, which we described above, and which can result in the greatest loneliness.

§2. The Missionary Poverty of the Companions of Jesus

We live in a consumer world. It is also a world of flagrant injustices and scandalous economic inequalities, one where affluence and wealth can become stumbling blocks for us. The Gospel can never be effectively proclaimed in such a world unless it makes clear its challenging and beckoning power to those who want to turn their backs on riches and come to know the liberty needed to serve the Lord Jesus with fidelity.

It is Christ's poverty that mobilizes Ignatius of Loyola's disciple to take on a life of poverty and self-abandon. This poverty is described in two key meditations in the *Spiritual Exercises* "The Kingdom of Christ" and "The Two Standards." It is the impoverished Lord who enables the disciple to discover that the person who does not possess the goods of this world is not necessarily cursed. Instead of being a curse, privation is just the opposite; it is a way, a source of blessing.

The Society of Jesus does not always give a visible indication of poverty. The many institutions it uses for its apostolate—the high schools, universities, retreat houses, churches, residences—all of these often make the Society seem as if it is a corporate real estate magnate. Alongside this question of maintaining institutions, which has become important during the past twenty years or so, there has also been a conscious effort made to appear less pretentious, less conspicuous.

Moreover, there has been a movement led by some Jesuits which, even though it has not had a direct bearing on the whole Society, has been successful in some places. These Jesuits are bent on changing the corporate image of the Society; or more exactly, they have been calling for a break with the traditional way Jesuits live—even in those countries which have been Catholic for centuries. The Thirty-second General Congregation chose to make "solidarity with the poor" a characteristic of the life of all Jesuits, and this option for the poor has found an echo in countries throughout the world. But "solidarity with the poor" will never be realized in fact unless there is an increase of the kind of places where Jesuits can share their lives with the poor, with those economically underprivileged people who make up a quarter of the world's population.

The logic of such a policy as legislated by the Congregation is integrated into all of the apostolic works undertaken by the Society of Jesus. But the fact that the Society owns or operates well-established institutions is not seen as so great a concern as the spirit which animates these institutions. What kind of people do these institutions serve? What kind of teaching is offered by them as a result of the Society's decision to have apostolic preference for solidarity with the poor? Service of the faith and the promotion of justice should not be considered as two lines that will eventually converge, but rather as two inseparable aspects of the Jesuit's priestly ministry in today's world.

There are two meditations from the *Spiritual Exercises* that help put into clearer perspective the tension that the companions of Jesus may feel exists between the demands of apostolic efficiency and apostolic poverty. This is a false, illusory tension, and we should try to put it to rest. In the "Principal and Foundation," Ignatius asks us to consider creation's law, the law which teaches a man how he is to live and love. Here we learn to recognize that ultimately every creature can be a means for us to praise, reverence, and serve God. Then, in "Three Kinds of Humility" we focus on Christ poor and humble. The purpose of this meditation is to move our hearts to make a thorough renunciation of all types of riches. The lesson of the first meditation is that Jesuits should use the material goods and institutions placed at their disposal as means in their apostolic work; in the light of, and according to the spirit of, the second meditation, they should feel themselves called to living in a more complete type of poverty so that they identify with the poor through whom the Lord today yet makes visible the unseen and suffering radiance of his glory.

It was this twofold "logic" that the Thirty-second General Congregation attempted to articulate in a very general way by recalling the distinction St. Ignatius had clearly made between the colleges (institutions for apostolic work) and the "professed houses" (communities for Jesuits engaged in the mission, that is the apostolate).[3] In its Decree on Poverty, the Congregation regulated that from now on there ought to be a clear distinction made between the budgets and revenues of the apostolic works in which Jesuits are engaged and the communities of the Society. The former should be governed by some

---

[3]In order to understand the importance Ignatius placed on the poverty of the "professed houses," it is enough to remember, as we read in that part of his "Spiritual Journal" which is extant, the long discernment (40 days) which he gave to this question before finally deciding that no fixed revenues should be sought or possessed either by these houses or by the churches attached to them.

directives of poverty (the chief of which should be based upon the relationship of means, however modest, with the end to be achieved), and the latter regulated by another criterion, namely love for the poor Christ and the determination to imitate Him and be in reality more like Him.

It is because he is a religious and a missionary that the Jesuit desires to live a life of actual poverty. He hears the advice Jesus gave his apostles when he sent them to announce the Kingdom of God: "Take nothing for the journey."[4] And, especially this reflection which places the apostle in the very heart of the mystery of God Himself: "You received without charge, give without charge."[5] The Word the apostle receives is priceless, and yet it was given to him by the Lord of the Gospel with open-handed liberality. The love Jesus showed, the sacraments He gave us, everything He did during his stay on earth—all of this simply witnesses to the same infinite generosity of our God. For the Companion of Jesus, who feels overwhelmed by so much goodness and who sees in his own vocation a gift that throws in relief the incomprehensible goodness of the Lord, the only choice possible is this: to give back everything, including himself, in the same way, not counting the cost, not calculating the conditions, but sharing Christ's liberating message with all the poor of the world and with men who await salvation. My ministry consists simply in preaching Christ's message truthfully. So, how can I expect to be remunerated when I lay out before others His message, which is devoid of all pretense and self-seeking? "You received without charge, give without charge." When I give freely, "without charge," I penetrate even deeper into the gratuity of the Word, into that gratuity which becomes enfleshed when it is communicated and accepted. The result of my giving in this way is that the Word, which has now come to me as His grace, intensifies His grace-giving work in me by showing me the universality of the gift which He has given to me. I have been gratuitously given my vocation as a Companion of Jesus and my ministry as His apostle. What if I used these gifts for greedy purposes? What if I reneged on the desire I once had to lose my life, not to hold on to it? How false my life would become. How I would muzzle His

---

[4] Luke 9:3.

[5] Matthew 10:8.

Word. How grossly I would pervert its meaning. What a loss of what was at one time beginning to be realized in me.

I can be sincere in accepting a "compensation" for a ministry performed only if I take what is offered to me in imitation of God's generosity. I should be able to see how this generosity is reenacted through what my brother does for me, that is through the spontaneous gift of his stipend. When he receives the Word through me, is he not moved to divest himself of something so that he can share it with me? In his offering does not he in turn discover for himself the gratuity of this Word of which I am but the dispenser?

For this reason, the Companion of Jesus exercises his priestly service to others without any preoccupation about what he "makes" in the ministry. He regards the community of his brothers, where everything is held in common, as the place of sharing and he does not attempt to learn who is responsible for bringing in what resources. Rather, in the community where as a poor man in companionship with his brothers, he lives out his life of consecration to Him who during the course of His life chose to be poor; he finds the opportunity to bury himself even deeper in the poverty of the world, in the place where the heart of the poor Christ, the source of love and salvation for all, continues to beat.

As far as institutions and other functions of the apostolate are concerned, the Companion of Jesus should recall the patently clear advice St. Ignatius gave on how these should be put to use for the service of others. Ignatius counseled that the Jesuit ought to be ready to use all human means without ever placing his full confidence in any of them.[6] He should therefore be careful not to allow himself to be tricked by the mirage of riches and power, even when he uses these in the service of others. He knows exactly that these are only a means and he should not consider any means except in relation to the apostolic end for which they are called on to serve. He also realizes that confidence should be placed in God alone. It is God who confounds the strong and proud of heart, and it is He who also will make it His business to bless those works which appear, at first sight and from a human point of view, to lack ordinary, reasonable and even essential means for success.

---

[6]*Constitutions* [814], 332-33.

§3. Mutual Witness to the Lord's Presence

A person living in community will entertain feelings of affection and love for those with whom he lives, and he will want to manifest these spontaneous feelings in his dealings with them. Of course, his commitment to chastity continually purifies his heart from the slightest things which could compromise or destroy it in this matter. The kind of purity of heart that results from steadfast celibacy grounds a man in humility, consideration for others, and mutual esteem for everyone. Ignatius took up the matter of how a Companion of Jesus was to deal with others in the third part of the *Constitutions* where he wrote specifically about those who were still in formation. He expressed his ideas on this subject with a certain solemn austerity in the following text. At first reading, it might appear that he discourages any spontaneous interaction with others. Of course, he does not. Apart from that, what he says does indeed underline the essential conditions for every type of community life.

> All should take special care to guard with great diligence the gates of their senses (especially the eyes, ears, and tongue) from all disorder, to preserve themselves in peace and true humility of their souls, and to give an indication of it by silence when it should be kept and, when they must speak, by the discretion and edification of their words, the modesty of their countenance, the maturity of their walk, and all their movements, without giving any signs of impatience or pride. In everything they should try and desire to give the advantage to the others, esteeming them all in their hearts as better than themselves [Phil. 2:3] and showing exteriorly, in an unassuming and simple religious manner, the respect and reverence befitting each one's state, in such a manner that by observing one another they grow in devotion, and praise God our Lord, whom each one should endeavor to recognize in his neighbor as in His image.[7]

The person who lives in community is not an abstract individual; he is a flesh-and-blood man. Abstract *intentions* are not enough to build together a community life that gives praise to God by actual

---

[7]*Constitutions* [250], 155.

demonstrations of true charity. All of man's senses and each of his organs, especially the eyes, ears and tongue, are potential sources for either causing trouble or building a brotherhood where the Lord's presence is felt. My way of seeing and hearing, of speaking or of keeping silent—these can vitally affect the climate of my community life. Experience, with the findings she has garnered, can be the best adviser on how to answer the following questions: Why do I continue to act in a way that hurts my brother or prevents him from being what he is meant to be? Why do I always capture center stage thereby hampering others from acting and from achieving their potential? Why, when others expect some communication from me, do I wrap myself in a cloak of unsociable silence? The "Examination of Conscience," which Ignatian spirituality encourages me to make on a regular basis, offers me the opportunity to rectify whatever there is in my conduct that makes life difficult for others and to correct my unsociable actions to conform to the sensibilities of the men with whom I live.

It is clearly obvious that whenever men live together in community, impatience and pride may stand out in opposition to honesty and peace. They prevent me from accepting someone else as he is and encourage me to claim a place of honor for myself. Whenever I act in this way, I go contrary to the Gospel which promises the first place to the last.[8] But I should not be eager to "give the first place to others" in hopes of receiving some reward. No, it is out of a sincere conviction, the result of the way I see others and of the knowledge I have of myself, that I am led to consider them superior to myself. This conviction makes me more attentive to their virtues than to their defects and it makes me all the more determined to take the beam that prevents me from seeing clearly out of my own eye than to remove the splinter I see in the other's eye.[9]

The text cited from the *Constitutions* referred to having "respect and reverence" for the other. These terms show us that our basis for action does not owe its rationale to the criteria of this world. Respect and reverence have their source in the Lord's presence in each one of my brothers. Jesus' way of acting can serve here as an example. He was more disposed to become enraptured by the good he saw in

---

[8]Luke 14:7-11.
[9]Matthew 7:3-5.

man's heart than to commiserate with him because of his wretchedness and his need for salvation.

We stated that these recommendations from the *Constitutions* were intended for the young Jesuit in his formation period. But these same attitudes, which the young Jesuit is invited to implement in his life right now and which little by little are meant to be inscribed in the simple daily routine of the community, are also intended to prepare him for being the apostle of tomorrow.

It is not merely toward the brothers with whom I live that I should show humility and attentiveness, patience, and respect. Putting aside selfishness and every form of arrogant self-seeking should not be limited to life in the Jesuit community. What is essential for my life in the apostolate is a thorough change of my feelings and emotions, a transformation modeled on the example of Jesus "meek and humble of heart."[10] Like poverty and obedience, the vow of chastity that the Jesuit makes has its own special resonance in the success of his apostolic vocation. What has the Companion of Jesus chosen through his vow of chastity? Consecration of his life to Christ and the opportunity to love Christ, as well as a readiness to be open in a fraternal way to every encounter animated by Christ's name. This is the meaning of his being a celibate. It is completely the opposite of being cut off affectively to wither in a desert of self-sufficient isolation. The grace of the companion's vocation is essentially linked to his determined participation in the Lord's mission. His priestly heart is formed after the pattern of the Good Shepherd as Jesus described him in the Gospels.[11] How could the companion ever reach out and know the sheep, much less make himself known to them, how could he ever be ready to lay down his life for them, if he had not over a long period of time fostered within himself an ability to listen to them with unstinted attention and interest; if he had not first learned to recognize the grandeur of God and His work in each and every one of Jesus' brothers; if he had not tried by every means possible to put down tendencies of self-seeking and desires to possess and dominate, and unless he had conquered all the rest of the selfish emotional inclinations he recognized within himself? When Jesus chooses him for the work of building up His kingdom, He does not tamper with his heart, but He does teach it to beat in unison with His own.

---

[10]Matthew 11:29.
[11]John 10:11-14.

§4. "Paternal" Government

If we reintroduce here the subject of obedience in our reflections on the Society's apostolic corps, which is what this chapter is supposed to be all about, it is only because St. Ignatius considered obedience the first and most important element in his order. As a matter of fact, the missionary spirit and the apostolic life of the Society of Jesus are rooted in obedience. It is in the "account of conscience" the Jesuit makes to his superior that he lives out existentially the total surrender of himself and his work to the whole apostolic corps of which he is a member.

At this point, then, we should take a look at how the Society is centrally organized and attempt to understand why such is the case. There are more than 26,000 Jesuits spread throughout the world, and although they belong to a number of different provinces and local communities, they are all members of one single corps.[12] The superior general has personal jurisdiction over each and every one of them. Of course, it is only rarely that he uses this authority in a direct way; however, he does so when his decision about a man or a community is deemed of great consequence.

It is for this reason that when a Jesuit finishes his formation and is engaged in the apostolic life of the Society, that is, when he is ready to be admitted into the Society publicly and definitively, it is up to the superior general to call him to "last vows." Then, too, whenever a provincial superior or a local superior of a major or large community has to be appointed, it is again up to the superior general to make the assignment. Understandably, in order to speed up the process in such cases as these and others like them, each superior must send regular up-to-date progress reports to the general in Rome on the activities of the order in his particular province. Through these reports the correspondent furnishes the general with detailed and ongoing information about the mission. In this way the peripheral life of the Society keeps itself united to the central office. Moreover, both the general himself and his assistants and consultors multiply these contacts with the provinces by conferring with superiors and men in

---

[12][TRANSLATOR'S NOTE: The number of Jesuits has continued to decline since the publication of this work. As of January 1, 1990, the official total number of Jesuits throughout the world is 24,421. "Supplementum Catalogorum Societatis Iesu, 1991": Romae: Apud Curiam Praepositi Generalis, 30 Septembris 1990.]

charge of different works of the Society at the province level whenever they make their frequent visits to Rome.

From the purely human point of view and, one might say, from
the point of view of company management, the order's administration is exceptionally active and efficient. However, to examine merely
the external, well-oiled administrative machinery that keeps the
Society going, is to get stuck at a superficial level and to end up not
understanding the spirit behind all these reports and efficiency.

Governance in the Society of Jesus is essentially "paternal." This
means that governance is either downward, from headquarters to the
field or upward, from the field to headquarters—if such a description
could ever really define the essence of a brotherhood where all
authority is regarded as a means for being of service to others and all
relations between superiors and subjects are seen as personal ex-
changes. Furthermore, I not only offer all of my work, abilities, and
talents to God in the Society of Jesus, but I give Him my whole self,
everything I am. For this reason every decision my superiors make
that concerns me affects my whole self. The Society's policy of
governance reflects this fact. The flow of information which circulates
from the periphery to the center and from the center to the periphery
covers a wide assortment of subjects, for example: projects to be
undertaken (including the resulting financial consequences of all
options under consideration), the mode of living in communities,
and the apostolic works in which various communities are engaged.
This ongoing tide of information makes it possible to come to a
realistic evaluation of all the elements surrounding some particular
work to be achieved in any mission by the particular men who are on
hand to see it through. As for the "sanctification" of these men, isn't
the aim here of both the apostolic mission and the individual's vocation the same? However, such a highly centralized organization
would fall short of realizing the purpose of its existence if its government were based on something other than this continuous in-
terchange of information between headquarters and the field and if
it were not built around a mutual knowledge and confidence of both
the superior and the rank and file. In this context the "account of
conscience" each Jesuit gives to his superior plays a vital role. The
account should not be seen as something observantly rendered during
the course of a formal meeting with the superior. Rather, each Jesuit
lives out this ongoing conversation of obedience with his superior
during the course of his whole life, and whenever the changing

circumstances of his life invite him to open himself to his superior, he should do so. What is important for me is that I should not live my life cut off from everyone else, as if I alone were responsible for carrying out my mission. Once I open myself up to my superior about what affects me, how I live, what I look for and hope to accomplish, the subjective element in my commitment becomes drawn up and joined to those aspirations of the entire Society; it becomes part of the larger apostolic endeavors exercised by the whole corps.

There have been times during the past few years when the term "responsible" has been used instead of the term "superior." The argument has been that some might take "superior" to mean a man endowed with higher qualifications and thereby might obscure the real meaning of the apostolic fraternity, which the Society truly is. On the other hand, the term "responsible" could connote that those responsibilities which ought to be assumed by every Jesuit and by the community as a whole are concentrated in one man. It is precisely because the centralized government of the Society of Jesus is a personal government; that is to say, it is a government that addresses itself to persons, it combines a very large admixture of co-responsibility in its policy of governance. The ordinary rank-and-file Jesuit is expected to act like a man by taking on his responsibilities with a keen sense of duty and personal initiative, and he is expected to carry out what those responsibilities entail. The ties that bind him to the local community, the province, and the whole order give him not only the right but even the obligation to speak up to his superiors about what seems to him best for the Society and his particular apostolate.

In our first chapter we discussed what was required for community spiritual discernment and what it was that makes this practice difficult to realize. Community spiritual discernment is the formal way of magnifying to community scale everything which gives structure to making the ongoing dialogue of obedience between the individual Jesuit and his superior possible. When the Jesuit tells his superior about those things that affect his life and his work, he informs him at the same time about his questions, reactions, and hopes; and he does so in a way that goes far beyond what is of immediate concern to him and his particular job. By this fact alone he shows his interest in the whole corps as well as in the local and provincial communities into which the whole corps is divided.

The unbroken tradition of the Society of Jesus requires that before the superior give his judgment on a particular matter, he consult widely all those who may be able in any way to shed light on different questions touching the matter at hand. This same tradition provides the superior with a group of consultors whose office it is to question him on all the important points of his governance.

Today the principle of subsidiarity is evoked with great frequency whenever the subject of government in religious orders and congregations arises. Jesuits put this principle of subsidiarity to use as a matter of policy. When a Jesuit is assigned a mission, the superior relies on that man's sense of responsibility for carrying out his job. As a member of the Society I can see the different tasks I am expected to do when I am assigned to a particular mission. I know that, when my superior gives me a general task to perform, he expects me to use my common sense as a Christian and a religious. For this reason I do not run back-and-forth asking him to make the decisions that are up to me to make. Of course, because I want to live in obedience, I am happy to tell him later how I carried out the job. If I am the superior and ask one of my brothers to be responsible for taking on some job, I know that he will use industry and prudence to see it through, and so I am not going to worry about telling him exactly what to do. Doubtless he can do the job better than I could anyway. But it is only because we have conversed openly with one another and because he has confidently told me about his life and work that I, in turn, through questions and reactions, can show that I have confidence in him.

Ultimately it is God who calls each man and entrusts him with his mission under the direction of his superiors. The man responds with his whole self. As a consequence of this choice, the brotherhood of the Society carries on its mission under the direction of its superiors, who have the care for the common good on the personal, communal and apostolic planes and whose governance should be circumspect and fully trustworthy.

§5. The "Image" of the Superior

For the reasons given above, the superior in the Society of Jesus cannot exercise his authority in an arbitrary manner. He has not been invested with an absolute and discretionary power. There is no place for the potentate, nor even for the sovereign in this order whose external structure conjures up the adjective "monarchical." This is so because each member of the Society has been invested with the responsibility of the conscientious steward in the Gospel.[13] For those who wish to live as Companions of Jesus, the "king," "landowner," "master" can be no one other than Jesus Himself. Moreover, the purpose of obedience is realized on the part of the one who obeys to the extent that he obeys what his superior commands "just as if it were coming from Christ our Savior"[14] and, on the part of the one who gives the orders, to the extent that he manifests in his own person Christ's way of thinking, feeling, and acting.

Ignatius takes up the subjects of "the Society's head" and "the government descending from him" in the Ninth Part of the *Constitutions*, and he develops this theme in a number of pages dedicated to the character and role of the Society's superior general. Jesuits like to see the features of Ignatius himself in the portrait he has painted of the general in chapter two, where he gives a brief list of the essential characteristics designed to serve as normative for all superiors in the Society of Jesus, irrespective of the level on which they exercise authority.

The first of the "qualities which are desirable in the superior general," addresses itself to the man's interior life.[15] He should be closely united with God our Lord, and intimate with Him in prayer, and action. If such a close union is not there, how can he possibly exercise in the Lord's name the responsibility which he has been given? How could he, aided by all of his companions, perceive, understand, and decide what will be for the glory of God and the greater service of the order in which he has a governing role?

The second quality found in this chapter from the *Constitutions* deals with the moral and spiritual qualities a superior should have. The first and most important of these is that he should be a man who edifies his brothers by his "example in the practice of all virtues." The term "edify" or "edification" should be explained in this context. It does not mean the superior should be content to give his brothers a kind of external encouragement by his conduct; the etymological meaning of the term is denoted in this context. The superior is

---

[13]Matthew 25:14-30.

[14]*Constitutions* [547], 247.

[15]Ibid. [723], 309.

expected to build up the corps of the Society and encourage its growth by giving it strength and vitality. Among all the "virtues" recommended, there are two for which he should be conspicuous because these two express externally the superior's interior attitude toward God and neighbor. Ignatius has expressed it in this paragraph: "Charity should be especially resplendent in him toward all his fellowmen and above all toward the members of the Society; and genuine humility too should shine forth, that these characteristics may make him highly lovable to God our Lord and to men."[16]

Ignatius continued to sketch the superior's moral profile when he stressed the fact that he should give evidence of having interior freedom, that he manifest composure and have a tight control of all his passions. An integrated, well-balanced man, he should be able to overcome different types of subjectivism and exercise his reason with a sufficient guarantee of objectivity. He should have such control over his own feelings that he will not allow them to show in what he says, acts, or does, and he will avoid all contacts that could prevent him from being a man for each and every man. For Jesuits as well as for "externs" he will be irreproachable in this matter, creating respect and confidence, supporting and encouraging in each one whatever is just and good.[17]

When it comes to exercising his office, the superior will, on the one hand, avoid the arguments of persons who could create obstacles to "the rectitude and severity" needed to realize the objective good of the men who have been entrusted to him and the objective good of their mission. But, on the other hand, he should manifest love and "tenderness" toward those dependent on him, and "kindness and gentleness" should be clearly conspicuous in his dealings with them. This way the superior will be without reproach and will accomplish his duties without compromising in any way the objective good of the mission or the personal good of those entrusted to him. "Thus, if they are being reprimanded or punished, they will recognize that in what he does he is proceeding rightly in our Lord and with charity, even though it is against their liking according to the lower man."[18]

16Ibid. [725], 309-10.
17Ibid.
18Ibid. [727].

Ignatius rounded out the portrait of the superior's moral and spiritual qualities by speaking more explicitly in this part of the *Constitutions* about the virtues of "magnanimity and fortitude of soul." Fortitude to act, staying power in contradictions, composure in success as well as in adversity—these are the required virtues for a man whose office gives him responsibility in an apostolic order. These particular virtues are needed more in some circumstances than in others. The superior therefore ought to be strong, solid, a man of unwavering courage, who can persevere in difficult situations, who will not give up before threats, and who will not give in to temptations of self-satisfaction or discouragement.[19]

The third part on this triptych of the moral qualities for a superior in the Society is dedicated to the man's intellectual endowments. These gifts refer less to a proved competence in some specialty of knowledge than to those gifts, both natural and acquired, that become evident in his administration. A knowledge of the Church's ordinary teaching is indispensable here. This is so, even if the superior has ready access to the enlightened counsel of experts concerning the most delicate aspects of Church doctrine. But what one looks for even more in him are gifts of good judgment and prudence, the ability to discern the presence of the Spirit in giving successful remedies for both the exterior and personal problems presented to him.[20]

Following this quality is a summary of traits necessary for the man of action: "He should be vigilant and solicitous to undertake enterprises and be energetic in carrying them through to their completion and perfection, rather than careless and remiss in such a way that he leaves them begun but not finished."[21]

Finally, Ignatius lists some physical traits that a man should have in order to be able to do his work; then he gives necessary "extrinsic endowments," such as "reputation, high esteem, and whatever else aids toward prestige with those within and without."[22]

Thus, the portrait is finished. In a sense Ignatius has used a broad brush to paint an ideal. But there is not a single superior in the Society of Jesus who does not see that he himself is an imperfect image of the

---

[19]Ibid. [728].
[20]Ibid. [729].
[21]Ibid. [730], 311.
[22]Ibid. [731-33].

figure that Ignatius has so depicted. Nevertheless, the order in which Ignatius arranges the desirable qualities he sees as necessary in a superior reveals his specific vision for governance in the Society. He says that what is of paramount importance in the person who should be allowed to serve his brothers in the ministry of authority is the presence of spiritual and moral qualities. To these qualities are added seriousness of formation and clarity of judgment. These are the same qualities that will enable him to give direction to the work of a group of Jesuits, to animate a community, and to lead it faithfully to the grace received and in union with the whole corps.

Most certainly it will have to be the Lord's goodness and the brothers' forgiving spirit that will actually make up for all of the superior's personality gaps and defects. This same goodness and forgiveness will encourage each man in the community to keep his heart unprejudiced and generous, to cooperate unselfishly in the community's common mission and to dedicate all of his endeavors humbly to it. This he should do with respect for the assigned role each man has in the community and with complete confidence in God's governance which through all things and events reveals itself and succeeds in working out its purpose.

V

"For the Greater Glory of God"

§1. A Spirituality of Service

As we have pointed out in the first chapter, a religious order offers a particular understanding of the Gospel, highlights specific characteristics of the figure of Christ who is still at work today among His own, announcing and building up the Kingdom of God. The religious order is able to do this because it inscribes in the life of the Church a continuation of a grace given to its founder or group of founders.

A religious order, therefore, is a gift from the Spirit, a gift given to the Church. It is the continuing visible display of a grace that was first given to an individual man or woman, or to a group, who founded the order. It is not human design that brings a religious order to birth, nor is it today's members who give it its roots. Thanks to the power of the Spirit imparted to it, a religious order is fundamentally a preordained participator in a mystery hidden in God; from its very beginning and continuing down to the present time, it is a chosen role player in a divine mystery.

Every religious order is permeated by a spiritual quality, and it is this "spirit" that determines the manner of the order's participation in the "mystery" of God and of His covenant with His people. Of course, it is never easy to describe this quality. Too precise a definition of a religious order risks letting the complexity of its vital quality escape notice and an oversimplified formula betrays the reality of the living entity. Direct experience with the order gives us a better insight into what it really is. This is why we are not going to attempt to define in any conclusive way the spirituality of the Society of Jesus. Rather, it is our intention in this final chapter to limit ourselves to a description of the different facets of that spirituality and to offer some concrete examples of how it manifests itself. What we are going to say here will often repeat what we have already said in a variety of ways throughout the book. However, we will look at the Society of Jesus now more from a contemplative point of view from the inside out, searching to discover in God and in God's love the secret which Jesuits endeavor to receive as a grace. It is not our intention to treat everything here with an equal depth of viewing. Rather we hope throughout this chapter to supply those who have so far followed our attempt to trace "the way of the Society of Jesus" with a definite image of its mystery.

The element of service is intrinsic to the spirituality of Ignatius of Loyola and his companions. However, it would be a mistake to use the example of Martha as opposed to Mary to explain the meaning of this service.[1] In the *Spiritual Exercises* the meditation on the "Principle and Foundation" makes a point of showing how man and all other things on the face of the earth attain the end for which they were created by their relationship to God and to His first gift, that is to His presence and action in all created things. Man can only be what he is meant to be and to become; this means he cannot reach the fullness of his dignity if he does not bind his life to the service of God. Of course, such a service can assume very different forms. In the missionary spirituality of the Society, the figure of Jesus has an absolutely central place—to proclaim the Kingdom and to transform the world through the conversion of man's heart. We have already made reference a number of times in this study to chapter ten of St. Matthew's Gospel. It is here that the evangelist describes how poverty, mobility, and confidence are prerequisites for the apostolic mission. Today's Companions of Jesus see themselves as being sent into the world in the same way the apostles were sent. Service of God becomes the day-to-day reality for them, once they have become convinced that they are being sent among their brothers to proclaim the coming of the Kingdom and that their service is a mission that attempts to transform the world by calling it to a total conversion. Service is also lived out in their lives when they listen to the Word as Mary did; that is, listen actively and attentively to the one and only Word, "the true light that enlightens all men,"[2] so that they will be able to bear wit-

---

[1]Luke 10:38-42.
[2]John 1:9.

ness to this Word and to enflesh it into all the possible means at their disposal for carrying out the apostolate. This is the meaning of the Word revealed to us in Jesus, the Word who in His very activity— service to the Father and service to people—brings about reconciliation and covenant. To live a spirituality of service according to the missionary vocation of the Companion of Jesus is, therefore, to bind one's destiny to that of the Word, to suffer as He did, to be rejected, to look for ways to transform the world of man and the cultures of men as Jesus did; that is, by opening them up to receive God's gift.

It is for this reason that the spirituality of service is a Christ-forming spirituality. The call and desire formed in the soul of the companion who contemplates Jesus and His mystery in the meditation on the "Third Kind of Humility" in the *Spiritual Exercises* affirms that such is the case.[3] To serve means to take on the role of the servant, or rather, it means to choose Him as Master who was the first to assume willingly for our sake the role of the servant, and to offer Him our very lives so that He can clearly impress upon them His Gospel: "No servant is greater than is master."[4] "I am among you as one who serves."[5] It is only in the light of the death and Resurrection of Jesus that the life of service can be fully appreciated. The spirituality of service is both the gift and the loss of one's own life in order that that life can be given in abundance to one's brothers and sisters. Therefore, the spirituality of service is saying yes to the totally gratuitous life that God wants to give to all of His children in Jesus. It is forgetting self so as to live in remembrance of God; it is letting self go so as to be able to find self, to let oneself be found in that place where the lost sheep found refuge. This movement does not take its inspiration from within oneself, but rather from the Heart of the Father who, by sending His Son, willed to transform the face of the world through the power of the Spirit. It is therefore the spirituality that emanates from the love of the triune God.

---

[3]See Chapter 1, section 6.
[4]John 13:16.
[5]Luke 22:27.

§2. In the Love of the Trinity.

Ignatius of Loyola habitually used the preposition "with" when he wanted to describe the relationship between Christ's life and our own. (This same preposition *cum* appears in the term "companion.")[6] On the other hand, St. Ignatius seldom used the term *frater*, that is, "brother." To him Jesus was the Son and the Lord. We see a two-way direction in these two separate terms, Son and Lord. They make clear the relationship of Jesus to God and to man—a polarity we must see together, never separated into their component parts.

The respect—reverence, even—that Ignatius gave to the title "Lord" is striking. Of course, as we consider his usage we should keep in mind that in his younger years he had been a page, soldier, and courtier. But also we should consider what an affection is transparent on the countenance of the Master who has called into His service the converted *caballero*! Yet his closeness to the Lord during this conversion period at Loyola and Manresa is also combined with distance. And while Ignatius found himself mystically introduced into the experience of intimate communion with God, nothing was taken away from the grandeur and holiness of the One who called him and communicated with him. Jesus is the indispensable way for us to come to the Father. He is the beloved Son in whom the Father is well pleased, and in His most holy humanity He has made the loving-kindness and the compassion of the Father accessible to us. Yet, His Lordship manifests to us, sinners that we are, the very inaccessibility of God; and so, in going to Him and coming into His glory we need support of someone of our own humankind who can help us approach Him. We have need of our Blessed Mother, the Virgin Mary. Such are the incentives and "meditations" that animate the prayer of Ignatius. To some extent they explain his human mannerisms that he brought with him into the universe of God.

In responding to the voice of his beloved Lord, the Companion of Jesus lets his Lord form within him a heart like His own, that is, a heart which is filial and fraternal, capable of adoring and ready to accept any mission. The Holy Spirit, the source of love and the living

---

[6][TRANSLATOR'S NOTE: Companion is composed of "com" from the Latin *cum* "with" and "panion" from the Latin *panem*, "bread." A companion, therefore, is one who breaks bread with you, a "messmate."]

force of love, gives him the grace which enables him to respond humbly in his everyday life to God's first gift, that is, to the gift of His presence and His action, the gift of the ongoing revelation God gives him of His glory.[7]

We referred earlier in this work to a very important event in St. Ignatius's life that took place as he was on his way to Rome. At the village of La Storta he heard the call that he had heard the first time at his conversion. What lingered in his mind as the main point of this experience was, he confessed, that on this occasion "so clearly did he see God the Father was placing him with Christ, His Son, that he had no doubts that God the Father was placing him with His Son."[8] Each Jesuit shares this same experience. He knows the Father Himself gives him His Son as his companion; he realizes that from now on his life will not be measured solely by the beat of his own heart but rather by the gratuitous and immeasurable gift from Him who is the source of all good, and who has not only revealed His love by sending His beloved Son into the world, but who yet shows His incomprehensible compassion by enlisting in His mission of salvation, men who are so unworthy and sinful to be companions "with" His Son, sharing in His work, His suffering, and His glory. The mission of Jesus continues through these men and in their day-to-day mission. It is Jesus' Gospel they proclaim; it is His authority they exercise; it is His actions they duplicate. Such are the inexhaustible sources of grace and salvation, the principle of transformation of human existence, the strength of renewal for all those who lie helpless along the route, weary and dejected as sheep without a shepherd.

Just as Ignatius and his first companions knew how to open their hearts to a recognition of the nature of the grace that was given them, so too in his turn will each companion realize through the grace given him that his decision to serve does not owe its origin to himself, that it is not merely the result of his human availability to do God's work. Another will had to express itself and that Will is at work today in the depths of his heart. The sole certitude and assurance it gives him is "I want you to serve Us."[9]

---

[7]We are describing the movement that takes place in the contemplation proposed at the end of the *Spiritual Exercises*, that is in the so-called, "Contemplation to Attain the Love of God."

[8]Ignatius of Loyola, *A Pilgrim's Journey*, 133.

[9]Ibid.

The *Spiritual Exercises* recommend that the exercitant beg the Divine Persons for the grace to love; and he relies upon all the saints in heaven to obtain this grace for him. Therefore, the Divine Persons are not the only Ones to whom the Companion of Jesus is encouraged to address his humble and confident prayer. It is when he is at work, when he is straining all of his resources that he realizes that he is in communion with these saints as one sent by the Father to be with the Son to serve. The Spirit of God is able at this point to fill his heart with thanksgiving and adoration. The Spirit can guide him along earthly paths inspiring his most ordinary activities as well as his most heroic contests. The companion knows that his life is no longer solely his own, but it belongs to Christ who wants to continue to complete in him His mysteries, to continue to be the Savior of the world and of all men. His joy is to proceed along his way totally engulfed in the fire of the Holy Spirit, this fire which is not seen but which all the same inflames his heart and consumes his members, this fire of love which is the gift God gives to all men of good will.

§3. For the Greater Glory of God.

Before we begin to speak of the glory of God we should say something about the fire of God. In Scripture divine "glory" is this inaccessible, radiant Holiness whose presence was attested by the cloud which enveloped it. This holiness revealed itself to the prophets and seized them in such a way that they were completely absorbed in a mission not of their own making, a mission which exacted from them a total obedience.

But in the fullness of time this mission was revealed in an unexpected way, through the simple and humble life of Jesus of Nazareth, who appeared as the servant, a condition He did not hesitate to take on for our salvation.

"No one has ever seen God."[10] "Philip, anyone who has seen me has seen the Father."[11] So was wrought the passing from the old to the new covenant. God is still the God of all holiness and He requires that, in order for us to be reconciled to Him, we must pass through

---

[10]John 1:18.
[11]John 14:9.

the abyss of death and through the total abandon of one who assents to not possessing his life any longer but rather to receiving it fully as a gift. This is all disconcerting for man. Yet there is One of us who has already opened up this passage for us all. From the very depths of ignominy from where our sins plunged Him and from where now shines forth the dawn of the new creation, there is Someone whose death has revealed to us the purest act of love. In the light of the Risen Jesus all life—His but particularly our life—has become permeable to God's glory. This is the way the Apostle Paul saw it. After considering all the possible activities in which man can become involved, he had no hesitation about telling the Corinthians: "Whatever you eat, then, or drink, and whatever else you do, do it all for the glory of God."[12]

St. Ignatius of Loyola was moved by the same firm belief as Paul and so he came to see the same urgent need. No other expression had more meaning for him in summing up man's commitment than the "glory of God." Beyond those hoped for, and sometimes attained, results, which can be a recompense for a man's endeavors, there is another radiant light not part of the earthly horizon that shines forth, a new gleaming brilliance that indicates the divine finality, sanctity, and love—this means opening up human existence to a totally new breadth of vision.

When we look at Christ's filial obedience, the obedience He exercised in carrying out the Father's Will, the obedience through which He achieved communion with the glory of the Father, we contemplate the form in which the abandonment to glory and the reception of glory are expressed. Jesus Himself said: "Human glory means nothing to me . . . How can you believe, since you look to each other for glory and are not concerned with the glory that comes from the one God?"[13] God's glory is not to be compared with human glory. Human glory pays particular attention to appearances, never goes below the surface and has no effect on what it touches. On the contrary, God's glory transforms the spirit which is open to it and it achieves its purpose from within. It is the radiant illumination of the true, the brilliant luster of the good, the dazzling iridescence of love.

Because the Son obeys the Father from the inmost recesses of His being, the Father's glory becomes transparent in Him, and He reveals

---

[12] I Corinthians, 10:31.
[13] John 5:41-44.

who the Father is. From Father to Son, glory establishes the ineffable communion and all the gratuity of the Spirit; that is, the glory of love which each exists for the other and gives Himself to the Other without reserve. On the last evening of His earthly life Jesus prayed to the Father that this glory of love be fulfilled in Him, even unto death itself, the glory of love capable of receiving all, and of offering all, in the infinite exchange of the Spirit: "I have glorified you on earth by finishing the work that you gave me to do. Now, Father, glorify me with that glory that I had with you before ever the world existed."[14]

In Jesus, God's glory is completed; in the Paschal event—that is, in His suffering, death, and Resurrection—God and creation are definitively reconciled in the embrace of love between the Father and Son.

But for us who grope along our way and who contemplate the light only through darkness, God's glory is still a goal which remains partially inaccessible to us, one which mobilizes the impulse of our faith and sets us en route at every moment. The expression "for the greater glory of God," which is the usual way in English to sum up the *raison d'être* Ignatius gave to the Society and its works, does not say anything about the constant effort which our commitment to obedience implies in our conforming to Christ and His mission. Like the English rendition, the Latin expression, *Ad maiorem Dei gloriam* uses the comparative form, not the superlative. God's glory must grow, develop, "always become greater"! This is the imperative inscribed in the life and mission of Jesus, and for us Jesuits it must be achieved through our own filial and missionary obedience. The twofold purpose of the Society of Jesus—the sanctification of oneself and the sanctification of one's neighbor—therefore finds in God its very source, purpose, and final end: a glory of God which is always greater!

This same light puts into clearer perspective the twofold devotion traditionally fostered by the Society of Jesus—devotion to the Eucharist and devotion to the Sacred Heart of Jesus.

What is perpetuated in the Eucharist is God's measureless gift of love which goes beyond the unfathomable depths of sin and hatred to create an eternal communion between God and man, and between each man and his brothers and sisters, his fellow human beings. Is

---

[14]John 17:4-5.

not this how in a most improbable way the Lord of the universe makes the heart of the world constantly grow and vibrate? From where else can be born the divine glory, which is always becoming greater in our world, than from its primary source: the Body and Blood offered in the free obedience of Him who untiringly transforms our history into a history which is both fraternal and filial?

The Sacred Heart of Jesus, the visible image and symbolic expression of the infinite love of God, announces in the midst of the world the truth which saves and transfigures us all. "For this is how God loved the world: He gave His only Son so that everyone who believes in Him may not perish but have eternal life."[15] The glory of God, is it not man alive?[16]

§4. Contemplatives in Action

The religious (and every Christian, for that matter) who makes his life an act of communion with divine love is introduced by this same love to the heart of contemplation which renews his vision and allows him to discover the Presence and the Gift without which nothing could exist. God shows Himself before his eyes and He speaks to him in his heart. He fills up, or tries to fill up all the space, inside and out, wherein he moves and lives his life.

No one can close himself up in the contemplation of God without at the same time allowing himself to be led by God's own Word and to be guided by His own light. Jesus, the only Son of the Father, by the example of His life and attitudes, by His way of dealing with others, and by His actions leads us little by little to the discovery of God. By communicating the Spirit of the promise, He opens our eyes to that divine universe which we have borne within ourselves ever since our baptism, but which still must manifest its very own glory for us. In this way He attunes us to the action of salvation which permeates all of the happenings of our world so as to finally reconcile humanity with God.

---

[15]John 3:16.

[16]We cite here the well-known saying of St. Irenaeus: "The glory of God is man alive; moreover the life of man is the vision of God." *Adversus Haereses*, Book 4, ch. 2, paragraph 7.

The person whom God calls to integrate his life in song and praise, in reading and meditation, and in confronting solitude where God is to be recognized as the all-in-all for the fulfillment and the accomplishment of His glory, is a person who abdicates from actual apostolic action and from the immediacy of ministry, in the name of love for the ineffable One. He knows and believes that the Son is the unique messenger and minister of God; that salvation comes about through His life, death, and Resurrection; and that yesterday, today, and tomorrow God is fulfilling His everlasting covenant with His children.

Such is not, however, the prayer of the Jesuit. We have already indicated how Ignatius of Loyola's Spiritual Exercises opens up another way, one not opposed to, but different from, the prayer described above. The movement which permeates the Exercises leads the one who prays to embrace the most holy will of God by conforming his life to the mystery of Jesus, particularly to the mystery of His suffering, death, and Resurrection.

Ignatius had to struggle from the beginnings of the history of the Society with the tendency of some Jesuits to extend the time for prayer. It was not that the pilgrim of Manresa stood in opposition to lengthy prayers. Rather, this movement among some Jesuits that he had to curtail came from an erroneous conviction and a false teaching. Those who stood in opposition to him believed prayer could not be considered authentic unless it extended over a period of one or more hours. This view would have transformed the Society of Jesus into a contemplative order.

Ignatius took the stand he did because, in his eyes, going from contemplation to apostolic activities did not constitute a withdrawal from contemplation. The reason is that for him the union of a person's liberty with God's will leads him to a firm and courageous commitment to communion with God. But this communion comes about in a mission, a mission which is essentially the mission of Jesus. Moreover, it is in this mission that one pursues the gift of His presence and love through putting aside all self-seeking and through the total giving of self to the demands of proclaiming Jesus' Gospel.

No doubt the most common risk today is not from an excessive amount of time spent in formal prayer. It is from too much activity, which devours time and tends to obscure the person's inner world that is founded on total union of one's will with God. From the Ignatian perspective, the essential issue remains the same. Once when someone was praising one of the companions for his prayer, Ignatius ventured to ask if the man was truly a mortified man. He asked this question to verify the authenticity of his prayer. And so it is with apostolic generosity. Giving oneself unreservedly to the apostolate does not have its intended results unless its roots are planted deep in the type of abnegation the Son of Man lived when he offered His life for his brothers.

There is an expression by Jerome Nadal, one of the early interpreters of the Ignatian way, that tells well what the unity between prayer and apostolic action should be in the life of the companion who has been taken in hand by his Lord and guided by Him toward the total gift of himself. That expression is "Contemplative in Action." Another maxim, this one from St. Ignatius, describes well how these two principles should be integrated in practice: "Find God in all things and all things in God." It is certain, to say the least, that this phrase is not found at the beginnings of the road along which the Spiritual Exercises invite one to commit himself to follow. Rather it is found at the end. The world of the "old man," encumbered as it is with anxieties, selfish interests, and desires, ought to be exchanged more and more for the true world, the world of God, the world where one risks not being accepted, where one's talents may not be recognized, yet where the Kingdom reveals itself and grows. The apostle who contributes to the building up of this Kingdom must have his vision enlightened by prayer and honed through prayer to see the presence of Jesus in his life. It is essential for him to understand and to love in God the work he has dedicated himself to without reserve. And he must do so without any measurement of his own personal success or his all too human perceptions, but rather with an unlimited hope in God alone. The Jesuit prays to revitalize his love, to express his thanksgiving, to become the interpreter before God for all his brothers. It is in this prayer, this encounter where the living Word of God continually tells him over and over again the truth of his faith and enlightens not only his whole life and his desires but also the life and desires of the world. It is in his prayer that he must also learn for himself once again that he is sent where the Kingdom beckons him to go—to a commonplace work which has no apparent importance or to a work charged with glamour eliciting recognition from men. His prayer teaches him to be strong in this certitude: If God calls him and communicates Himself to him in His Son Jesus, and if He sometimes lets him experience the impulse of love from the Holy Spirit, it is because he himself and the world are saved by his opening himself more and more to this divine Presence.

Ignatius seems to have a preference for one type of prayer above all others—at least for Jesuits. This is the examination of conscience.[17] Let us not think of the examen, as it is also called, as an expression of a moralistic conception of the spiritual life. As it is understood and practiced in the school of Ignatius, the examination of conscience is totally contrary to a practice where the judgment of right and wrong behavior is the ultimate frame of reference. The examen considers what is happening in one's life, but it is always conspicuous because it stresses these points: giving thanks to God, being receptive to his light, considering in this same light one's own life, asking for His pardon, and expressing a desire to grow in love. In a life given over completely to God and to the mission of his Son for the salvation of the world, the constant repetition of this mental attitude expressed in the examination of conscience joins together one's personal history with divine grace. The Jesuit can then offer humbly this history to the transforming action of the Holy Spirit.

§5. In Sickness and in Death

Both during his whole life and also and even more at the time of his death, each member of the Society ought to strive earnestly that through him God our Lord may be glorified and served and his fellowmen may be edified, at least by the example of his patience and fortitude along with his living faith, hope, and love of the eternal goods which Christ our Lord merited and acquired for us by those altogether incomparable sufferings of His temporal life and death.[18]

---

[17]In that part of the *Constitutions* that deals with young Jesuit students (scholastics) and the understandably limited time they have to give to prayer, we read that they are nevertheless advised to make the examination of conscience twice a day: "Consequently, in addition to confession and Communion, which they will frequent every eight days, and Mass which they will hear every day, they will have one hour. During it, they will recite the Hours of Our Lady, and examine their consciences twice each day, and add other prayers according to the devotion of each one until the aforementioned hour is completed, in case it has not yet run its course." *Constitutions of the Society of Jesus*, [342], 184.

[18]*Constitutions* [595], 264–65.

This text from the *Constitutions* allows us to complete our reflection on "the way of the Society of Jesus" in the definitive light of the Paschal Mystery of Jesus, where we are given a glimpse of the glory of the Son of God.

Each stage in our life admits of a special way in which we are united in the mystery of the Lord. So the Companion of Jesus will come to know those moments when he is invited to conform in a privileged way, according to this circumstance or that, to the life and death of Christ. As we have explained, the scene of the Lord sending His apostles forth on a mission gives the best and most accurate illustration of the service Ignatius and his sons are called upon to give to the Church. And if this is the case, then the picture of the hidden life of Christ at Nazareth would best represent the years the Jesuit spends in formation; the final stages of his life, when he must pass from speech to silence, from a life bristling with activity to one of passivity and suffering, should find their meaning in the last hours in Jesus' life, that is, in His passion and death.

This is the time more for prayer than for rest. Every province of the Society of Jesus has a catalogue where the principal occupations of each man are noted, and there is a set formula printed after the names of those Jesuits who have reached this final stage: *Orat pro Ecclesia et Societate*. "He prays for the Church and the Society." If yesterday a Jesuit's apostolic comings and goings and the demands of his daily job prevented him from spending long hours in prayer, then today, during the evening of his busy life, he will find more time to spend alone with his Lord. In his adoring contemplation of Him who is the Way, the roads he has covered over the course of his life will come together more and more. His Lord is there, and by joining him to the mystery of His own suffering and death, He is waiting for the encounter, preparing to call His friend, His companion, to the Kingdom of everlasting light, of communion with the Father, Son, and Holy Spirit: "Well done, good and trustworthy servant; you have shown you are trustworthy in small things; I will trust you with greater; come and join in your master's happiness."[19]

---

[19]Matthew 25:21.

Appendix I
The Founding Text

On September 27, 1540, Pope Paul III issued the bull *Regimini militantis Ecclesiae* which gave the Society of Jesus its first official approbation. This bull incorporated the text of the "Formula of the Institute" (the "fundamental rule" of the order) written by Saint Ignatius.

On July 21, 1550 Pope Julius III reconfirmed the Society of Jesus in the bull *Exposcit debitum* which approved an edited version of the "Formula of the Institute." The text of this "Formula" is reproduced here.[1]

THE FORMULA OF THE "INSTITUTE" OF THE SOCIETY OF JESUS (1550)

1. Whoever desires to serve as a soldier of God beneath the banner of the cross in our Society, which we desire to be designated by the name of Jesus, and to serve the Lord alone and the Church, His spouse, under the Roman pontiff, the vicar of Christ on earth, should, after a solemn vow of perpetual chastity, poverty, and obedience, keep what follows in mind. He is a member of a Society founded chiefly for this purpose: to strive especially for the defense and propagation of the faith and for the progress of souls in Christian life and doctrine, by means of public preaching, lectures, and any other ministration whatsoever of the word of God, and further by means of the Spiritual Exercises, the education of children and unlettered persons in Christianity, and the spiritual consolation of Christ's faithful through hearing confessions and administering the other sacraments. Moreover, this Society should show itself no less useful in

---

[1] *Constitutions of the Society of Jesus* [3-6], 66-72.

reconciling the estranged in holily assisting and serving those who are found in prisons or hospitals, and indeed in performing any other works of charity, according to what will seem expedient for the glory of God and the common good. Furthermore, all these works should be carried out altogether free of charge and without accepting any salary for the labor expended in all the aforementioned activities. Still further, let any such person take care, as long as he lives, first of all to keep before his eyes God and then the nature of this Institute which he has embraced and which is, so to speak, a pathway to God; and then let him strive with all his effort to achieve this end set before him by God—each one, however, according to the grace which the Holy Spirit has given him and according to the particular grade of his own vocation.

2. Consequently, lest anyone should perhaps show zeal, but a zeal which is not according to knowledge, the decision about each one's grade and the selection and entire distribution of employments shall be in the power of the superior general or ordinary who at any future time is to be elected by us, or in the power of those whom this superior general may appoint under himself with that authority, in order that the proper order necessary in every well-organized community may be preserved. This superior general, with the advice of his associates, shall possess the authority to establish constitutions leading to the achievement of this end which has been proposed to us, with the majority of votes always having the right to prevail. He shall also have the authority to explain officially doubts which may arise in connection with our Institute as comprised within this Formula. The council [general congregation], which must necessarily be convoked to establish or change the Constitutions and for other matters of more than ordinary importance, such as the alienation or dissolution of houses and colleges once erected, should be understood (according to the explanation in our Constitutions) to be the greater part of the entire professed Society which can be summoned without grave inconvenience by the superior general. In other matters, which are of lesser importance, the same general, aided by counsel form his brethren to the extent that he will deem fitting, shall have the full right personally to order and command whatever he judges in the Lord to pertain to the glory of God and the common good, as will be explained in the Constitutions.

3. All who make the profession in this Society should understand at the time, and, furthermore, keep in mind as long as they live, that

this entire Society and the individual members who make their profession in it are campaigning for God under faithful obedience of His Holiness Pope Paul III and his successors in the Roman pontificate. The Gospel does indeed teach us, and we know from the orthodox faith, and firmly hold, that all of Christ's faithful are subject to the Roman pontiff as their head and as the vicar of Jesus Christ. But we have judged nevertheless that the following procedure will be supremely profitable to each of us and to any others who will pronounce the same profession in the future, for the sake of our greater devotion in obedience to the Apostolic See, of greater abnegation of our own will, and of surer direction from the Holy Spirit. In addition to that ordinary bond of the three vows, we are to be obliged by a special vow to carry out whatever the present and future Roman pontiffs may order which pertains to the progress of souls and the propagation of the faith; and to go without subterfuge or excuse, as far as in us lies, to whatsoever provinces they may choose to send us—whether they are pleased to send us among the Turks or any other infidels, even those who live in the region called the Indies, or among any heretics whatever, or schismatics, or any of the faithful.

4. Therefore before those who will come to us to take this burden upon their shoulders, they should ponder long and seriously, as the Lord has counseled [Luke 14:30], whether they possess among their resources enough spiritual capital to complete this tower; that is, whether the Holy Spirit who moves them is offering them so much grace that with His aid they have hope of bearing the weight of this vocation. Then, after they have enlisted through the inspiration of the Lord in this militia of Christ, they ought to be prompt in carrying out this obligation which is so great, being clad for battle day and night [Ephesians 6:14; 1 Peter 1:13].

5. However, to forestall among us any ambition of such missions or provinces, or any refusal of them, all our members should have this understanding: they should not either directly or through someone else carry on negotiations with the Roman pontiff about such missions, but leave all this care to God, and to the pope himself as God's vicar, and to the superior general of the Society. This general too, just like the rest, should not treat with the said pontiff about his being sent to one region or another, unless after advice from the Society.

6. All should likewise vow that in all matters which promote the observance of this Rule, they will be obedient to the one put in charge

of the Society. (He should be as qualified as possible for this office and will be elected by a majority of the votes, as will be explained in the Constitutions). Moreover, he should possess all the authority and power over the Society which are useful for its good administration, correction, and government. He should issue the commands which he knows to be opportune for achieving the end set before him by God and the Society. In his superiorship he should be ever mindful of the kindness, meekness, and charity of Christ and of the pattern set by Peter and Paul, a norm which both he and the aforementioned council [general congregation] should keep constantly in view. Assuredly, too, because of the great utility to the order and for the sake of the constant practice of humility which has never been sufficiently praised, the individual subjects should not only be obliged to obey the general in all matters pertaining to the Society's Institute but also to recognize and properly venerate Christ as present in him.

7. From experience we have learned that a life removed as far as possible from all infection of avarice and as like as possible to evangelical poverty is more gratifying, more undefiled, and more suitable for the edification of our fellowmen. We likewise know that our Lord Jesus Christ will supply to His servants who are seeking only the kingdom of God what is necessary for food and clothing. Therefore our members, one and all, should vow perpetual poverty in such a manner that neither the professed, either as individuals or in common, nor any house or church of theirs can acquire any civil right to any produce, fixed revenues, or possessions or to the retention of any stable goods (except those which are proper for their own use and habitation); but they should instead be content with whatever is given them out of charity for the necessities of life.

8. However, the houses which the Lord will provide are to be dedicated to labor in His vineyard and not to the pursuit of scholastic studies; and on the other hand, it appears altogether proper that workers should be provided for that same vineyard from among the young men who are inclined to piety and capable of applying themselves to learning, in order that they may form a kind of seminary for the Society, including the professed Society. Consequently, to provide facilities for studies, the professed Society should be capable of possessing colleges of scholastics wherever benefactors will be moved by their devotion to build and endow them. We now petition that as soon as these colleges will have been built and endowed (but not from resources which it pertains to the Holy See to

apply), they may be established through authorization from the Holy See or considered to be so established. These colleges should be capable of possessing fixed revenues, rights to rentals, or possessions which are to be applied to the uses and needs of the students. The general of the Society retains the full government or superintendency over the aforementioned colleges and students; and this pertains to the choice of rectors or governors and of the scholastics; the admission, dismissal, reception, and exclusion of the same; the enactment of statutes; the arrangement, instruction, edification, and correction of the scholastics; the manner of supplying them with food, clothing, and all the other necessary materials; and every other kind of government, control and care. All this should be managed in such a way that neither may the students be able to abuse the aforementioned goods nor may the professed Society be able to convert them to its own uses, but may use them to provide the needs of the scholastics. These students, moreover, should have such intellectual ability and moral character as to give solid hope that they will be suitable for the Society's functions after their studies are completed, and that thus at length, after their progress in spirit and learning has become manifest and after sufficient testing they can be admitted into our Society.

Since all the members should be priests, they should be obliged to recite the Divine Office according to the ordinary rite of the Church, but privately and not in common or in choir. Also, in what pertains to food, clothing and other external things, they will follow the common and approved usage of reputable priests, so that if anything is subtracted in this regard in accordance with each one's need or desire of spiritual progress it may be offered, as will be fitting, out of devotion and not obligation, as a reasonable service of the body to God.

9. These are the matters which we were able to explain about our profession in a kind of sketch, through the good pleasure of our previously mentioned sovereign pontiff Paul and of the Apostolic See. We have now completed this explanation, in order to give brief information both to those who ask us about our plan of life and also to those who will later follow us if, God willing, we shall ever have imitators along this path. By experience we have learned that the path has many and great difficulties connected with it. Consequently we have judged it opportune to decree that no one should be permitted to pronounce his profession in this Society unless his life and doctrine have been probed by long and exacting tests (as will be

explained in the Constitutions). For in all truth this Institute requires men who are thoroughly humble and prudent in Christ as well as conspicuous in the integrity of Christian life and learning. Moreover, some persons will be admitted to become coadjutors either for spiritual or temporal concerns or to become scholastics. After sufficient probations and the time specified in the Constitutions, these too should for their greater devotion and merit, pronounce their vows. But their vows will not be solemn (except in the case of some who with permission from the superior general will be able to make three solemn vows of this kind because of their devotion and personal worth). Instead, they will be vows by which these persons are bound as long as the superior general thinks that they should be retained in the Society, as will be explained more fully in the Constitutions. But these coadjutors and scholastics too should be admitted into this militia of Jesus Christ only after they have been diligently examined and found suitable for that same end of the Society. And may Christ deign to be favorable to these our tender beginnings, to the glory of God the Father, to whom alone be glory and honor forever. Amen.

Appendix II
Vocation Directory

This is a listing of the locations of English-speaking vocation directors in North America; for information, please address your inquiry to "Director of Vocations" at the location in your area.

California

Jesuit Community
Loyola Marymount University
P.O. Box 45041
Los Angeles, CA 90045-0041
213-338-7445

Chicago

Provincial Offices
2050 N. Clark Street
Chicago, IL 60614
312-975-6363 (Office)
312-883-0499 (Residence)

Detroit

Loyola House
2599 Harvard Road
Berkley, MI 48072
313-399-8132

Maryland

Jesuit Community
Georgetown University
Washington, DC 20057
202-687-8989 (Office)
202-687-8086 (Residence)

Maryland

Leonard Neale House
1726 New Hampshire Avenue, NW
Washington, DC 20009
202-387-1481

Missouri

Provincial Offices
4511 West Pine Boulevard
St. Louis, MO 63108-2191
314-361-7765

New England

Provincial Offices
P.O. Box 799
Back Bay Annex
Boston MA 02117-0799
617-266-7233 (Office)
617-536-8440, Ext. 406 (Residence)

New Orleans

Provincial Offices
500 S. Jefferson Davis Parkway
New Orleans, LA 70119
504-821-0334 (Office)
504-865-2200 (Residence)

New York

Provincial Offices
501 E. Fordham Road
Bronx, NY 10458
212-584-0300

Oregon

Jesuit Novitiate
2222 N.W. Hoyt
Portland, OR 97210
503-226-6977

Wisconsin

Jesuit Novitiate
1035 Summit Avenue
St. Paul, MN 55105-3034
612-224-5593

Jesuit Conference

Secretary for Formation
Suite 300
1424 16th Street, NW
Washington, DC 20036
202-462-0400 (Office)
202-387-5375 (Residence)

Canada

P.O. Box 160, Station V
Toronto, Ontario
Canada MGR 3A5